ETHNIC CHRONOLOGY SERIES
NUMBER 25

# The Ukrainians in America
## 1608-1975
## A Chronology & Fact Book

Compiled and edited by

## Vladimir Wertsman

**1976**
OCEANA PUBLICATIONS, INC.
DOBBS FERRY, NEW YORK

# TABLE OF CONTENTS

EDITOR'S FOREWORD

Ukrainian Americans comprise an ethnic community of about
2,000,000 people spread all over the United States. The Ukrainians
were known and recorded in the past under different names: Rusyns,
Ruthenians, Rusniaks, and Little Russians, as well as under regional
names such as Carpatho-Russians, Lemkos, Boykos, Hutsuls, Galitzians,
Bukovinians. Heavier concentrations of Ukrainian Americans can be
found in the states of New York, New Jersey, Pennsylvania, Illinois,
Michigan, and Ohio. About two-thirds of Ukrainian Americans are of
Catholic (Eastern Rite) faith. The rest is predominantly of Eastern Orthodox faith. There are also some Protestant groups. Ukrainian Americans have a strong feeling of national and cultural identity.
They are hard workers, modest, creative, and made important contributions to our country especially in the fields of agriculture, engineering, science, architecture, movies, and sports. Dr. George
Kistiakovsky and Dr. Michael Yarymovich in science, Branko Nagurski
and Chuck Bednarik in sports, Anna Sten and Jack Palance in the
movies, are just a few examples from a list of numerous prominent
Ukrainian American personalities who are going to be met in this
book.

This volume was conceived to furnish essential information on
Ukrainian Americans. It contains a chronology of significant events
in the life of Ukrainian Americans, important documents related to
the events, an annotated bibliography broadening the sphere for future research, an appendix of Ukrainian American institutions and
organizations, influential periodicals, American colleges and universities offering courses in Ukrainian, and statistical tables.
Although intended primarily to serve as an introduction to reference
materials for secondary school and community college students, the
book should prove a valuable aid to teachers, scholars, researchers,
and other readers interested in ethnic studies.

In writing this book I have received the help of the Brooklyn
Public Library, Columbia University Library, Harvard University
Research Institute, Immigration History Research Center, University
of Minnesota, New York Public Library, Shevchenko Association, Ukrain-
ian Institute of America, and the Ukrainian Workingmen's Association.
I am especially indebted to Dr. Walter Dushnyk, managing editor of
the Ukrainian Quarterly Review, Professor Wassyl Lew, Mr. Jerry
Pronko, managing editor of the Forum: A Ukrainian Review, and Dr.
Alexander Sokolyshyn, senior librarian Brooklyn Public Library, for
their outstanding help and permission to reprint materials included
in the documents section. I am also grateful to my good friends
Anna Boychuk, Arline Cohen, Martin Dooley, Barbara Ann Watters, and
Paul Zaplitny for their splendid cooperation.

Vladimir Wertsman
Brooklyn Public Library
Brooklyn, New York

iv

| 1608 | Ivan Bohdan, the first Ukrainian in America, came together with the legendary Captain John Smith to Jamestown, Virginia. Before sailing for America, Captain John Smith fought in Eastern Europe against the Turks, fell prisoner, and later fled from captivity through the Ukraine, Romania, Hungary, and other countries. It is assumed that during this period, Smith met Bohdan and persuaded the latter to come to the New World. |
|---|---|
| 1658-1662 | Several Ukrainians, who were persecuted by the Polish Catholic Church and temporarily found refuge in Holland and Germany, emigrated to America together with Dutch and German colonists and settled in Pennsylvania. This is attested by records of the time which mention pure Ukrainian names such as Petro Luh, Hawrylo Gasha, Petro Kradly. |
| 1662 | The first Ukrainian who came to New York City was Albert Zaboriwsky. He was an immigrant from Holland. |
| 1775-1783 | Ukrainian Americans actively took part in the Revolutionary War for Independence. In the register of George Washington's army one can find such names as Petro Polyn, Mykola Bizun, Ivan Lator, Stephen Zubley, and many other Ukrainian names. |
| 1784 | The Russians founded their first settlement in Alaska at Three Saints Bay, Kodiak Island, and brought among the settlers many Ukrainian Cossaks from Siberia. |
| 1812 | The Russians founded Fort Ross colony, near San Francisco, California, and settled it with several Ukrainian Cossaks, who initially resided in Alaska, along with Russians and Alaskan Indians. |
| 1814 | March 14. Taras Shevchenko, the greatest Ukrainian poet and fighter for an independent Ukraine, was born. Shevchenko was a close friend of Ira Alridge, the famous black American actor, and dreamed of an American type democracy for his native country. Shevchenko's birthday is a Ukrainian national holiday celebrated by Ukrainian Americans as well as Ukrainians from all over the world. |
| 1861-1865 | A large number of Ukrainian Americans took part and bravely fought in the Civil War on President Lincoln's side. I. H. Yarosh, Petro Semen, Julius Koblansky, and several others gave their lives for the Union's cause, while Ivan Mara, Andrey Ripka, Joseph Krynicky and others distinguished themselves as officers. |
| 1868 | March 1. Reverend Agapius Honcharenko, a Ukrainian |

American intellectual and activist of San Francisco,
California, published <u>Alaska</u> <u>Herald</u> <u>and</u> <u>Svoboda</u>, the
first Russian, English, and partly Ukrainian newspaper
in the United States.  It was a bi-weekly publication
designed to bridge the cultural gap between the Russian and Ukrainian groups from Alaska and California,
and the rest of the English speaking citizens of the
United States.

1870s        The first wave of Ukrainian mass immigration to the
United States began.  The immigrants came mostly from
the Carpatho-Ukraine (Western Ukraine), Galicia (Poland),
and territories which were under Austro-Hungarian rule
at that time, and were driven from their native places
by precarious economic, social, and political conditions.

The newly arrived Ukrainian immigrants, mostly peasant
farmers of Catholic faith, settled heavily in or around
Philadelphia, New York City, Pittsburgh, Boston, Hartford, Buffalo, Newark, Chicago, Milwaukee, Detroit,
St. Louis, San Francisco and Los Angeles.  They came
with a desire to work, to be free, and to be able to
preserve their national heritage.  Many Ukrainian immigrants took hard jobs in coal mines, while others
engaged in farming, and cultivated Ukrainian wheats
such as Kharkov and Turkey read.

1884         Reverend Ivan Volansky, an immigrant Catholic priest,
arrived in Shenandoah, Pennsylvania, and devoted himself to the organization of Ukrainian American religious and social life.  For his numerous contributions to the development of Ukrainian American communities, as an indefatigable organizer, religious,
cultural, and social leader, Volansky earned the name
of "Father of Ukrainian Americans."

1885         December 19.  The first Ukrainian Catholic church in
the United States, St. Michael the Archangel, was completed in Shenandoah, Pennsylvania, under the direction
of Reverend Ivan Volansky.  Besides this church, Volansky directed and supervised the errection of churches
in Kingston, Olyphant and Shamokin, Pennsylvania, Jersey City, and others during the following years.

St. Nicholas Brotherhood, the first Ukrainian American organization, was founded by Reverend Ivan Volansky in Shenandoah, Pennsylvania.

1886         August 15.  <u>America</u>, the first Ukrainian newspaper in
the United States and the world, was published in
Shenandoah, Pennsylvania, by Reverend Ivan Volansky.

He was assisted by Volodymyr Semenovich, editor, and Vasyl Sarich, typesetter. The newspaper appeared for only one year.

**1887**   The first Ukrainian American choir was organized by Volodymyr Semenovich in Shenandoah, Pennsylvania. It soon was followed by several other choirs organized by different Ukrainian American communities.

**1889**   Reverend Ivan Volansky was recalled from the United States by his superiors from Lviv, Poland, under the pressure of Vatican authorities influenced by Latin Rite American Catholic bishops. The conflict was generated by the fact that Reverend Volansky belonged to the Eastern Rite Catholics, and defended the formation of Catholic parishes on the basis of ethnic origin. Eastern Rite Catholics had a married clergy and viewed the formation of Ukrainian parishes as a means of preserving the Ukrainian heritage, while the Latin Rite Catholics required celibacy for their priests, and opposed the organization of separate Ukrainian Catholic parishes.

**1890**   Ukrainian Protestants from Kiev, Ukraine, immigrated to the United States. The Protestant immigrants belonged to the Stundinsts sect, a Baptist denomination, and left their native country because of religious persecutions. The Stundinsts, about 2,500 families, first settled in Virginia, but later moved to North Dakota and founded a community called Kiev, named after the capital of their native country.

Ukrainian mass immigration from Bukovina, a province under Austro-Hungarian rule at that time, began.

**1891**   The conflict between the Ukrainian Catholics and the American Catholic bishops deepened. As a result of the refusal of Bishop John Ireland of St. Paul, Minnesota, to accept Reverend Alexis Toth, a Catholic priest from the Carpatho-Ukraine, into his diocese, Toth left the Catholic church. He switched to the Russian Orthodox Church, and started a campaign to convince the Carpatho-Ukrainians to accept the Russian Orthodox Church.

**1892**   The Union of Greek Catholic Brotherhoods in North America was founded as a fraternal organization by several Ukrainian American priests, and reunited about 50,000 members. It started publishing a weekly called <u>Viestnik</u> <u>Greko</u> <u>Kaft</u> <u>Sojiedinenija</u> (Greek Catholic Union Messenger) which is still in existence and has a circulation of about 18,000.

1893          The first Ukrainian language parish school was estab-
             lished in Shamokin, Pennsylvania.

1894          February 22. The Ukrainian National Association, the
             largest Ukrainian American organization, was founded
             in Shamokin, Pennsylvania by Gregory Hrushka. It pro-
             vides life insurance and supports various cultural,
             social, and recreational activities. Its main organ
             is Svoboda Ukrainskyi Shchodennyk (Liberty Ukrainian
             Daily), the oldest Ukrainian newspaper in the United
             States. It covers Ukrainian social, religious and
             cultural life in the United States, as well as inter-
             national news.

             Dissident members of the Union of Greek Catholic Bro-
             therhoods, mainly immigrants from Galicia (Poland), left
             the Union and founded the Ruthenian National Associa-
             tion.

1895          The Russian Orthodox Catholic Mutual Aid Society of
             U.S.A. was founded as a fraternal benefit life insur-
             ance organization, reuniting mostly Carpatho-Ukrainians
             who switched from the Catholic to the Russian Orthodox
             Church.

             Dr. Konstantin Sudzilovsky (Russel) a physician who
             initially settled in San Francisco, California, went
             to Hawaii and helped organize the medical society.
             Under his influence, about 365 Ukrainian workers left
             California for Hawaii.

1896          The Ukrainian National Association began publishing
             popular books in order to elevate the cultural level
             of its members.

1897          The Sisterhood of St. Olga was founded in Jersey City,
             New Jersey. It was the first Ukrainian women's organi-
             zation in the United States.

             The Russian Orthodox Catholic Mutual Aid Society of
             U.S.A. started putting out Svit (The Light) a semi-
             monthly written in the Carpatho-Ukrainian dialect and
             mostly devoted to Lemko history and Lemko communities
             news. Lemko is the province from which the Carpatho-
             Ukrainians emigrated. (See 1895)

1899          At the end of the nineteenth century, which coincided
             with the end of the first period of Ukrainian mass im-
             migration, it was estimated that about 100,000 Ukrain-
             ian Americans settled in the United States.

1900          The second wave of Ukrainian mass immigration to the
             United States took place. It lasted until the out-

break of the First World War, and the influx brought
about 250,000 new immigrants. They settled mainly in
or around the old centers of settlement.

July 1. The Russian Brotherhood Organization was
founded in Shenandoah, Pennsylvania, by Carpatho-
Ukrainians. It started publishing Pravda (The Truth),
a monthly publication concerned mostly with the Brotherhood's structure and development. The Brotherhood
is still in existence and serves as a life insurance
organization for its 12,000 members.

1901

February 10. Dr. Konstantin Sudzilovsky (Russel) was
elected to the Hawaiian Senate and made presiding of-
ficer. He was instrumental in passing a homestead law
benefiting 365 Ukrainian workers who resettled from
California to Hawaii. (See 1895)

1902

A church convention held in Harrisburg, Pennsylvania,
demanded the creation of a separate Ukrainian Catholic
diocese in America uniting all Eastern Rite parishes.
(See 1891)

Sokil (Eagle) and Sich, two gymnastics organizations
for young Ukrainians in America, were founded.

1903

Ukrainian Presbyterian groups were established in Newark, New Jersey, Pittsburgh and McKees Rocks, Pennsylvania.

1904

The Ukrainian National Association founded the A. Bonchevsky Publishing House and published many books destined for adult education courses. It also organized
evening schools and libraries in different centers.

1905

Peter Jarema organized the United Ukrainian Organization of New York City with the purpose of coordinating
various activities of different Ukrainian American
groups.

A Ukrainian Baptist congregation was established in
Scranton, Pennsylvania. Later, congregations belong-
ing to the same denomination were founded in Chicago,
Illinois, and Chester, Pennsylvania.

Ukrainian Protestants founded the Ukrainian Evangelical
Alliance of North America and started publishing
Yevanhelisky Ranok (Evangelical Morning), a bi-monthly
devoted to religious and educational topics.

St. George's Ukrainian Catholic Church was founded in
New York City.

1907          The Vatican appointed Stephen Soter Ortynsky as bishop
              of the Ukrainian Catholic Church in America. The ap-
              pointment of a Ukrainian bishop, as desired and de-
              manded by the increasing number of Ukrainian Catholic
              parishes and priests in America during several decades
              of immigration, was a victory for the Ukrainian Ameri-
              can Catholics. The Ukrainian bishop remained, however,
              under the control of the local Latin Rite hierarchy.
              (See 1902; see also 1889)

              A Ukrainian progressive workers organization called
              Haidamaky was organized in Trenton, New Jersey.

1909          A cultural congress dealing with Ukrainian language
              schools decided to publish Ukrainian textbooks and
              children's books in the United States. The congress
              took place in Philadelphia, Pennsylvania.

              A Ukrainian Presbyterian parish was established in
              Newark, New Jersey.

              The Ukrainian American Citizen's Association was found-
              ed in Philadelphia, Pennsylvania.

1911          The Ukrainian Workingmen Association was established
              in Scranton, Pennsylvania. It is still in existence
              and serves as a fraternal benefit life insurance com-
              pany. Its organ, Narodna Volya (The People's Will)
              continues to appear as a weekly with an English sup-
              plement.

1912          The Providence Association of Ukrainian Catholics in
              America was founded as a fraternal life insurance so-
              ciety. It started publishing Ameryka (America), the
              only Ukrainian Catholic daily, covering national and
              international news, as well as religious events and
              news of special interest to Ukrainians. Presently,
              the society has a membership of about 20,000.

1913          The Vatican, bowing to the continuous demands of Ukrain-
              ian Catholics in America, established a Ukrainian ex-
              archate making all Ukrainian Catholic parishes a separ-
              ate administrative church unit subject only to the Pope
              in Rome. Bishop Soter Ortynsky and all his succesors
              received the same rights as all American Catholic
              bishops. At that time, the Ukrainian Catholic exar-
              chate encompassed more than 200 parishes. (See 1907)

              The poet and scientist Alexander Neprytsky-Granovsky
              settled in the United States and published several col-
              lections of valuable poems in Ukrainian.

              Alexander Archipenko, world famous Ukrainian American

sculptor, was represented for the first time in this
country at the Armory Show in New York City.  Archipenko exhibited four works, of which "The Boxing Match"
was the most important.

1914      The Ukrainian National Aid Association of America was
created in Pittsburgh, Pennsylvania.  It is still in
existence, and serves as a fraternal life insurance
company for about 8,000 members.

St. Nicholas Ukrainian Catholic Cathedral was completed
in Chicago, Illinois.  The building has thirteen domes,
splendid Byzantine style paintings, window decorations,
and a capacity for more than 12,000 people.

1915      A group of Ukrainian Orthodox believers established
an independent Ukrainian People's church in Chicago,
Illinois.  It marked the beginning of a movement tending to create an all-American Ukrainian Orthodox Church
independent of the Russian Orthodox Church.

The Ukrainian National Council was established with
the aim of coordinating the Ukrainian American organized life.

The Ukrainian National Aid Association of America
started publishing a bi-weekly called Ukrainske
Narodne Slovo (Ukrainian National Word) shedding
light on the activity of different Ukrainian American
organizations.  One section is written in English.

Rosalia Rolenka of Detroit, Michigan, began teaching
Easter egg painting.  This type of painting, known as
one of the old Ukrainian traditions, became a recognized art, popularized in our day by Yaroslava Surmach-
Mills, a noted artist and teacher of New York City.

The first Ukrainian gymnastic society was organized
under the name of Sichovy Striltsy (Sich Riflemen) in
New York City by Peter Zadoretzky.

1916      The Sichovy Striltsy gymnastics society changed its
name to Sich Organization of Ukrainians in the U.S.A
and moved its headquarters from New York City to Chicago, Illinois.  Sich members organized festivals of
physical education and became well known all over the
country.

The United Russian Orthodox Brotherhood of America
started the publication of Russkij Vestnik (Russian
Messenger), a Carpatho-Ukrainian bi-monthly devoted
to important religious and social events in the
parishes.

May 6.  Reverend Agapius Honcharenko died at the age
of eighty-four in Haywards Hill, California.  Honcharenko's life and achievements in the United States
were described by many American newspapers and inspired
biographical works.  (See 1861)

1917        Misionar (Missionary) started to be put out as a monthly publication of the religious group called Sisters
of St. Basil the Great, located in Philadelphia, Pennsylvania.

The United Societies of U.S.A., a Carpatho-Ukrainian
fraternal benefit organization also known under the
name of Sobranie (Congress), published Prosvita (Enlightenment), with the aim of promoting organizational
interest.  The publication is still in existence, and
it has an English section.

March 16.  President Woodrow Wilson proclaimed the date
of April 21, 1917 as a day "upon which the people of
the United States may make such contributions as they
feel disposed to aid the stricken Ruthenians (Ukrainians) in the belligerent countries."  President Wilson's
proclamation was issued after the United States Congress discussed the matter at the request of Ukrainian
Americans, and adopted a resolution supporting the
Ukrainian cause.

1918        January 22.  The Ukrainian Rada (State Council) proclaimed the Ukrainian National Republic as a free,
independent and sovereign state, terminating three centuries of Russian subjugation.  A year later on the
same date, Western Ukrainian regions, previously under
Austro-Hungarian rule, were united with the Ukrainian
National Republic.  The birth of an independent and
united Ukrainian state was fully supported by Ukrainian Americans, who remained strongly attached to their
native country and fought for its independence.  The
Ukrainian National Republic had a short existence and
tragic end, but the date of January 22 remained Ukrain-
Independence Day, and is celebrated yearly by Ukrainian
Americans and Ukrainian communities from other countries
alike.

The American Ruthenian National Council was founded
with the objective of protecting and promoting the
special interests of Carpatho-Ukrainians who came from
the Western Ukraine.

1919        The Ukrainian Orthodox Church of the U.S.A. was founded
at a convention held in New York City.  It attracted
many Ukrainians who were members of the Russian Orthodox Church, and progressed under the able administra-

tion of Archbishop John Teodorovich.  Presently it is
the strongest and most numerous Ukrainian Orthodox
body in the United States having about 90,000 members
and more than 100 churches.

1920    After the defeat of the Ukrainian National Republic,
and the occupation of the Ukraine by Soviet Russia,
Ukrainian immigration to the United States slowed
down in comparison to the beginning of the twentieth
century.  Most of the immigrants were from the Carpatho-
Ukraine (Western Ukraine), and during the following
two decades, only about 40,000 new Ukrainian American
immigrants were recorded.  This influx marked the
third wave of Ukrainian mass immigration to the United
States.  (See 1900)

Ukrainski Visti (Ukrainian News), a leftist weekly,
was started by a pro Communist group.  It is still in
existence, but has a reduced circulation and influence
among Ukrainian Americans.

1922    The Union of Ukrainian Evangelical Baptist Churches
was formed with the aim of consolidating various Ukrainian Protestant parishes.  (See 1905)

Professor Aleksander Koshetz, a noted composer and director, and the famous Ukrainian National Chorus came
to the United States and successfully toured the country.  The chorus popularized the Ukrainian songs among
Americans, and contributed to the spread of Ukrainian
tradition among Ukrainian Americans.

Dr. Stephen Timoshenko, a specialist in the field of
theoretical and applied mechanics, elasticity and vi-
bration, settled in the United States.  He served on
the faculty of the universities of Michigan and Stanford, California, and published several scientific
works.

May 16.  The Ukrainian Technical Institute was established as a polytechnical school in New York City.

1923    Sculptor Alexander Archipenko settled in the United
States, and his works soon attracted the attention of
critics and connosseurs, who recognized in the sculptor
a valuable representative of the new art of sculpto-
painting, uniting form and color in an harmonious
assemble.

Igor Sikorsky, an aeronautical engineer born in Kiev
(Ukraine), formed the Sikorsky Aero Engineering Company, which produced the S-29, the first twin-engined
plane made in America.  He later organized the Sikorsky

Manufacturing Corporation, which built the S-38 flying boats and other aviation models.

**1924**

The Vatican approved the organization of two Ukrainian Catholic exarchates, and appointed two bishops, one for the Ukrainians who came from Galicia ) Poland), and one for the Carpatho-Ukrainians who came from the Western Ukraine. (See 1913)

The Trident Savings and Loan Association was founded in Newark, New Jersey.

The first Ukrainian theater was established in New York City under the direction of Ivan Dobriansky, but the theater lasted only one year. Another theater, a music hall founded by I. Havoronsky in New York City, lasted until 1928.

**1925**

George Chylak was elected mayor of Olyphant, Pennsylvania, and held this position for five years.

The Ukrainian National Women's League of America was founded in Philadelphia, Pennsylvania. It is the largest Ukrainian women's organization, non-sectarian and non-partisan, and presently has a membership of about 8,000. It sponsors cultural and educational activities as well as home economics.

The Ukrainian National Association decided, at a convention held in Rochester, New York, to publish a monthly magazine in English. It was the first step towards a bi-lingual publication, reflecting the increasing demands of the second generation Ukrainian Americans.

Veterans of the Ukrainian National Armies formed an organization called Striletska Hromada (The Riflemen's Community). The members of the organization were former military men of the Ukrainian National Republic who fought against Soviet Russia as well as other invaders. (See 1918)

St. Basil's school in Philadelphia, Pennsylvania, became the first Ukrainian Catholic all day school in America.

**1926**

The Ukrainian Orthodox Church of St. Volodymyr was established on East 14th Street in New York City.

The Russian Consolidated Mutual Aid Society was founded as a fraternal life insurance company by a group of Carpatho-Ukrainians.

George Kistiakovsky, a distinguished research chemist, came to the United States, studied at Princeton University, New Jersey, and later joined the faculty of Harvard University, where he became famous for his contributions in science.

1927    The Ukrainian Businessmen's Association was founded in New York City.

A group of Carpatho-Ukrainians of Yonkers, New York, started the publication of Karpatska Rus (Carpathian Rus) featuring articles on Lemko history, culture, and religion. It later became the official organ of the Lemko Association.

The Ukrainian Baptist Convention in the United States started the publication of Pislanets Pravdy (Messenger of Truth), a bi-monthly devoted to religious, educational, and other subjects of interest to church members.

The Federated Russian Orthodox Clubs was founded by several clubs of mostly young Carpatho-Ukrainian men and women belonging to the Russian Orthodox Church. The Federation, which presently has more than 5,000 members, sponsors various cultural, religious, athletic, and charitable activities and publishes The Russian Orthodox Journal, a monthly covering topics of interest to the members.

1928    The Ukrainian Orthodox Church in America was founded by Ukrainians who emigrated from Galicia, Poland, and Bukovina, Russia, and were former Catholics. Presently this Church has thirty-seven churches with a membership of about 40,000.

1929    The Lemko Association was founded as a fraternal and cultural organization of Carpatho-Ukrainians. It is still in existence and puts out two publications: Karpatska Rus (Carpathian Rus), a weekly, and Lemko Youth Journal, a bi-monthly. (See 1927)

1930    The first Carpatho-Ukrainian program in our country was broadcasted on the WMBQ station of Brooklyn, New York.

The Ukrainian Orthodox Church Club of Boston, Massachusetts, won two prizes for embroidery and costumes at the Boston tercentenary colonial costume ball.

Branko (Bronislav) Nagurski, a famous football player during the thirties, joined the Chicago Bears team, played tackle and brilliantly raised the team from ninth place to third place in the league. In the next years,

Nagurski won a place on the all-league team, three times consecutively.

The Ukrainian Chorus of Chicago, Illinois, directed by Leon Sorochinsky, won the first prize at the Chicagoland music festival. The same prize was awarded to the Chorus the next year.

Oznaky Nashoho Chasu (Signs of Our Time), a religious publication dealing with the interpretation of the bible, was published by the Pacific Press Publishing Association of Mountain View, California. It is still active.

1931

April 26. Vasile Avramenko's dancing school with about 300 Ukrainian American dancers gave a spectacular public performance at the Metropolitan Opera House of New York City. It was highly acclaimed by the press as the most outstanding musical performance of the year.

Anna Sten (born Stenski-Sujakevich), a leading movie actress, made her debut in Trapeze and The Brothers Karamazov, followed by Nana. She successfully appeared in several other movies during the next two decades.

Igor Sikorsky built the S-40, the first large American four-engined flying clipper. (See 1923)

The Organization for the Rebirth of Ukraine was founded as a Ukrainian nationalist organization sponsoring cultural, educational, and welfare activities.

During the 1931/1932 musical season, eighteen radio stations broadcasted Ukrainian programs, mostly sponsored by Surma Book and Music Company of New York City. The company is still active on the lower east side in New York City.

1932

Professor Alexander Koshetz and noted choreographer Vasile Avramenko successfully led Ukrainian American singers and dancers in a concert honoring the 200th Anniversary of the birth of George Washington in Washington, D. C.

Steve Halaiko and John Jadick, two noted boxers, dominated the pugilistic rings with their performances. Halaiko became a member of the United States Olympic team, while Jadick won the title of junior heavyweight champion.

Lawyer O. Malena won a seat in the Pennsylvania legislature.

Dmitry Chutro of Philadelphia, Pennsylvania, organized
a group of talented Ukrainian American singers who performed two Ukrainian operas: Zaporozhetz Za Dunaem
(The Cossak of Zaporozhe Beyond the Danube) and Mazeppa,
named after a 17th century leader of Ukrainian Cossaks.
Both operas were presented during two musical seasons
and were favorably received by musical critics.

1933        The Ukrainian National Youth Federation came into existence.  It united young people between the ages of
ten and fourteen promoting a Ukrainian nationalistic
orientation, as a youth branch of the Organization for
the Rebirth of Ukraine.  It also started a publication
called Molody Ukrainski Nationalisty (Young Ukrainian
Nationalists), which later changed its title to Trident Quarterly.

The Ukrainian National Association started publishing
The Ukrainian Weekly, an English supplement to the
newspaper Svoboda.

The Ukrainian Youth League of North America was founded
as an organization promoting athletic, educational, and
cultural purposes.  Its present publications are Trend,
a quarterly, and Trendette, a monthly, covering mostly
organizational news.  The League is non-denominational.

The Ukrainian Catholic Church in America organized the
Ukrainian Catholic Youth League, which later changed
its name to League of Ukrainian Catholics.

The Ukrainian Pavilion  at the World's Fair in Chicago,
Illinois, successfully featured Ukrainian sculpture,
architecture, cooking, folk art, and folk dancing.  It
had been the only pavilion fully supported by Ukrainian organizations or individuals from the United States
and other countries, without any government help.
Alexander Archipenko's works substantially contributed
to the success of the pavilion.

The Ukrainian Orthodox Church in America started publishing Ukrainskyi Pravoslavnyi Visnyk (The Ukrainian
Orthodox Herald), a quarterly devoted to theological
and educational topics of the church.

During the Ukrainian Week at the World's Fair in Chicago, Illinois, forty Ukrainian American and Canadian
professors met and discussed the possibility of founding a Ukrainian Academy of Sciences.

1934        The New York Association of Friends of Ukrainian Music
was founded.  It contributed to the popularization of
Ukrainian music in America.

The most successful concerts of the Ukrainian National
Choir, under the direction of Professor Alexander
Koshetz, were those given in honor of M. Haivoronsky,
a reputed Ukrainian American composer.

The Ukrainian Chorus of Chicago, Illinois, again won
the first prize at the Chicago music festival with
different ethnic groups participating. This time, the
chorus was directed by George Benetzky, a former tenor
of the American Opera Company.

1935    Witmark Educational Publications released twenty Ukrainian songs, including "Carol of the Bells" by Nicholas
Leontovych, a carol which became so popular that it is
considered a Christmas classic.

S. Jarema, a lawyer, won a seat in the New York State
legislature.

1936    Peter Fick, a noted Ukrainian American swimmer, was
selected for the United States Olympic team.

John S. Gonas won a seat in the Indiana State legislature.

Vasile Avramenko organized a Ukrainian film company in
New York City and produced two movies: Natalka Poltavka
(The Girl from Poltava) and Zaporozhetz Za Dunaem (The
Cossak from Zaporozhye beyond the Danube), using the
text of two Ukrainian classic plays.

Professor Alexander Koshetz successfully directed the
Ukrainian mixed choirs of the New York Metropolitan
area at Carnegie Hall, New York City. The concert,
the first of its kind in Ukrainian church music, presented to an American audience, was warmly received by
the public and musical critics alike.

1938    George Kistiakovski was promoted Abbot and James Lawrence Professor of Chemistry at Harvard University
after seventeen years of research on chemical reactions.

The American Carpatho-Russian Orthodox Greek Catholic
Church was founded by old Carpatho-Ukrainian immigrants
and their descendants. Presently this church has more
than 100,000 members and sixty-nine churches.

Severina Parylla, a Ukrainian nun, settled in the
United States and popularized the Ukrainian wood-
carving in this country.

A baseball league of The Ukrainian National Association
was established.

1939          Igor Sikorsky built the VS-300, the first successful
              helicopter produced in the Western hemisphere.

              Alexander Archipenko opened his own art school in New
              York City, where he taught until the end of his life.
              He proved to be a very talented teacher.  He also
              served as sculptor in residence at several universities
              around the country.

1940          May 24.  The Ukrainian Congress Committee of America
              was founded as a federation of anti-Communist organi-
              zations and was actively involved in the struggle for
              an independent and democratic state of Ukraine.

              Shlakh (The Way), a Ukrainian Catholic weekly, spon-
              sored by Apostolate, Inc., came into existence as a
              publication concerned with the national and religious
              education of the Ukrainians in the United States.

              The League of Americans of Ukrainian Descent was found-
              ed in Chicago, Illinois, as an organization helping
              to integrate Ukrainian immigrants in the American
              society.  It organized English courses for immigrants,
              offered welfare and counseling assistance, and parti-
              cipated in the Nationalities Fair of Chicago.

              The Ukrainian Garden, a section of the Cultural Gar-
              dens in Cleveland, Ohio, won the first prize for its
              architectural and esthetic arrangement.  The Ukrainian
              section had been planned and financially supported by
              the Ukrainian community of Cleveland, Ohio.  It has a
              statue of Volodymyr the Great, first Christian ruler
              of Ukrainians, and the busts of Taras Shevhenko, poet,
              and Ivan Franko, writer.  The sculptures were done by
              Alexander Archipenko.

1941          The Ukrainian Publishing Association started publish-
              ing Hromadskyi Holos (Voice of the Community), a bi-
              monthly pro-Communist publication devoted to Ukrainian
              political and social events.

              Mike Mazurki (born Michael Mazurski), a former heavy-
              weight wrestler, six feet and six inches tall, weigh-
              ing 245 pounds, made his debut in a Hollywood movie
              called The Shanghai Gesture, followed by Farewell My
              Lovely.  In the next decades he became a well known
              actor, appearing in several dozens of movies.

              Professor George Vernadsky, a reputed historian of
              Yale University, published Bohdan, Hetman of Ukraine,
              a work devoted to Bohdan Hmelnitzky, a legendary
              Ukrainian leader who fought against Polish oppression
              in the seventeenth century and tried to establish an

independent Ukraine.

1942      John Hodiak, a noted Hollywood actor, made his debut in the movie *Lifeboat*, together with Tallulah Bankhead. He later appeared in several other movies such as *A Bell for Adano*, and *The Harvey Girls*.

1943      Professor George Kistiakovsky became consultant to the Los Alamos Project, devoted to the creation of the atomic bomb. Later he was appointed as head of the explosives division of the Los Alamos Laboratory of the Manhattan Project.

Football player Branko Nagurski rejoined the Chicago Bears. He played tackle and helped the Bears to another world championship.

1944      June 20. The Ukrainian American Relief Committee was founded in Philadelphia, Pennsylvania, with the aim of providing assistance to new immigrants. This organization, which coordinates the work of 500 state and local relief agencies, played a very important role in resettling tens of thousands of Ukrainian immigrants after the end of the Second World War.

Professor Stephen Timoshenko became Professor Emeritus of Theoretical and Applied Mechanics at Stanford University, California. He was a member of the faculty staff for seven years and published several books on the theory of elasticity.

The Ukrainian National Women's League of America started publishing *Nashe Zhyttia* (Our Life), a monthly publication dealing with organizational aspects, as well as Ukrainian literature, folk art, and children. It also has an English section.

*Cerkovnyi Vistnik* (The Church Messenger) started to be published by the American Carpatho-Russian Orthodox Greek-Catholic Church as a semi-monthly concerned with religious topics and church news. The articles are written in the Carpatho-Ukrainian dialect, but with Latin letters. (See 1938)

The Ukrainian Congress of America started to put out *The Ukrainian Quarterly*, an English language publication, with special emphasis on the Ukraine. Besides articles on history, sociology, literature, ethnography, politics, etc., it also accorded attention to Ukrainian life in the United States. The publication is still in existence and has a circulation of about 5,000.

1945          During World War II, several thousands of Ukrainian Americans served with the United States Armed Forces, and hundreds of them were decorated for bravery in action. Among the most distinguished fighters, Nicholas Minue of Carteret, New Jersey, was posthumously awarded the Congressional Medal of Honour for a one-man attack and destruction of a German machine gun installation. Another hero, Lt. Colonel Theodore Kalakula, the first Ukrainian American graduate of West Point, was awarded the Silver Star and two oak leaf clusters for leading a daring attack against the Japanese after his company commander was wounded, as well as for saving important medical supplies during a Japanese air raid.

The fourth wave of Ukrainian mass immigration to the United States began. This wave, which lasted about a decade, brought 85,000 new immigrants from various concentration and displaced persons camps in Germany. They were victims of the Second World War and were substantially assisted by the United Ukrainian Relief Committee and the Ukrainian Catholic Committee of America. The new immigrants settled mostly in localities where Ukrainian communities were already established.

The fourth Ukrainian mass immigration brought an important number of professionals, skilled laborers, educated farmers, and a large segment of young people, who graduated from high schools or started college in Europe. Such a composition had a very healthy and beneficial impact upon the Ukrainian American community, the development of its organizations, press, cultural and artistic life.

Nicholas Malko joined the Chicago Symphony Orchestra, and remained its director for the next twelve years.

1946          June 15. The Organization for the Defense of Four Freedoms for Ukraine was founded in New York City. Since its inception, the organization published political literature and played an active role in coordinating meetings, protests or other actions aimed at defending freedom in the Ukraine.

1947          The Selfreliance Association of American Ukrainians was founded in New York City, with the objective of helping newly arrived immigrants, as well as assisting Ukrainian students. It presently has a membership of about 10,000, a library with several thousand volumes related to Ukrainian subjects, and conducts courses in Ukrainian literature and history.

November. The Shevchenko Scientific Society was founded in New York City as an institution supporting research

on the Ukraine and assisting immigrant Ukrainian scholars to adjust to their new life. The society, presently reuniting more than 400 members from different walks
of scientific life, writers and educators, organized
conferences, lectures, scientific sessions, and maintains a library and archives. It has several sections,
and publishes scientific papers, proceedings, memoirs,
almanacs, and works by different authors. The society
was named after Taras Shevchenko, the famous Ukrainian
poet.

The Organization for the Defense of Four Freedoms for
Ukraine started publishing Visnyk (The Herald), a
monthly shedding light on Ukrainian political life,
culture, historic events, and social issues.

Anatole Mazur joined the faculty staff of Stanford
University, California, as professor of history, and
taught this subject for the next two decades. He published Rise and Fall of the Romanovs, Russia: Tsarist
and Communist and other Russian historiography books.

The Ukrainian Autocephalous Orthodox Church (Soborno
Praina) was founded by a group of immigrants who did
not want to be under the administration of other Ukrainian Orthodox church bodies. Presently, they have a membership of only about 2,000 and four churches.

Bill Moisenko, Chicago's right wing hockey player, was
selected for the All Star Hockey Team in Toronto, Canada.

December 13. The Ukrainian Orthodox League was founded
in New York City, with the aim of promoting better
knowledge of the Ukrainian Orthodox faith, as well as
the Ukrainian national, religious, and cultural traditions.

1948      The Ukrainian Institute of America was founded in New
York City due to the patronage of Volodymyr Dzus, a
well-known Ukrainian industrialist. The institute
maintains a permanent exhibition of Ukrainian folk
arts, a Ukrainian historical gallery, and sponsors
lectures, conferences and concerts. It is also involved in philanthropic and educational activities.

The Ukrainian Engineer's Society was founded in New
York City for Ukrainian professional engineers, archi-
tects, and economists. Its aim is the promotion of
science and engineering.

Alexander Archipenko had his seventy-eighth one man
exhibition and brought forth his "modeling in light,"
with sculptures made of transparent and translucent

materials with light emanating from within.  (See 1939)

1949      The Ukrainian Bandurist Chorus was reorganized in
          Detroit, Michigan by Volodymyr Bozhyk and Hryhory
          Kytasty.  It is an all male chorus playing the bandura,
          a Ukrainian national instrument, and during the past
          decades it became a successful and outstanding repre-
          sentative of the Ukrainian choral tradition.  The
          chorus toured the United States, Canada, and several
          European countries.

          Jaques Hnizdovsky, noted woodcut master and graphic
          artist, came to the United States and established him-
          self in New York City.  His works were appreciated in
          the artistic circles, and many of them have been col-
          lected by libraries, museums, and private collectors.
          Hnizdovsky is represented in all major American museums,
          and even in the White House.

          The World Federation of Ukrainian Students Organiza-
          tions of Michnovsky was founded with the scope of pro-
          moting Ukrainian culture among university and college
          students and educators of Ukrainian descent.

          The Ukrainian Engineer's Society of America started
          publishing Visti Ukrainskykh Inzhineriv (Ukrainian
          Engineering News), a quarterly devoted to original
          research papers and technological and economical events
          in the Ukraine.  It also has a book review section.

          Ovyd (Horizon), a Ukrainian literary quarterly, was
          started in Chicago, Illinois, by Mykola Denysiuk.  It
          is still in existence and has a circulation of about
          1,200.

          The Ukrainian Literary Art Club was organized in New
          York City.  It conducted a special department in plas-
          tic arts, and soon similar departments were established
          by Ukrainian art clubs in Philadelphia, Pennsylvania,
          Detroit, Michigan, and in Canada.

          The Ukrainian chorus Dumka was organized in New York
          City with the purpose of promoting native Ukrainian
          songs.

          Charles Bednarik joined the Philadelphia Eagles foot-
          ball team, as center, and played with this team for
          the next thirteen years.

1950      Three Ukrainian American youth organizations were
          founded:  The Ukrainian Youth Association of America
          (SUMA) in New York City, Plast in Detroit, Michigan,
          and the Association of American Youth of Ukrainian

Descent in Maplewood, New Jersey. All three organizations operate summer camps and provide different cultural and recreational activities. The first two
organizations have a more pronounced political character, their aim is to defend the honor of the Ukraine
and to continue the traditions of Ukrainian fighters
for an independent Ukraine.

January 22. The Ukrainian Medical Association of North
America was founded as an organization for physicians,
surgeons, dentists, and other related professionals who
are of Ukrainian descent. It presently has a membership
of over 1,200 and provides scholarships for medical
schools, as well as a placement service. It also has
a library and medical archives.

The Ukrainian Academy of Arts and Sciences was established in New York City to sponsor and organize scholars
interested in the study of Ukraine. It has a museum
and library with more than 20,000 volumes on Ukrainian
history and literature, and interesting documents related to the history of Ukrainian immigration to the
United States. Shortly after its foundation, it started
publishing the Annals of the Ukrainian Academy of Arts
and Sciences, a scholarly publication, with materials
on Ukrainian history, literature, and social sciences.

New Ukrainian Baptist congregations were established
in Hartford, Connecticut, Cleveland, Ohio, Pittsburgh
and Philadelphia, Pennsylvania, and Los Angeles, California.

The Ukrainian Orthodox Church of the U.S.A. started
issuing Ukrainske Pravoslavne Slovo, a monthly conatin-
ing articles related to church organization and relig-
ous education.

The Organization for the Defense of Lemkivschyna published Lemkivski Visti (Lemko News), a monthly written
in the dialect of and devoted to the Ukrainians who
stem from the region of Lemkov, Poland.

Jack Palance (born Palaniuk), a leading actor with
stage experience, made his movie debut in the film
Panic in the Streets. He appeared in several other
movies during the next two decades, and received different awards.

1951          The Federation of Ukrainian Student Organizations of
              Michnowsky started publishing Feniks - Zhurnal Molodykh
              (Phoenix - Journal of the Young People), dealing with
              Ukrainian history, culture, politics, social sciences,
              as well as organizational news.

Edward Kozak started publishing Lys Mykyta (The Fox), a monthly satirical periodical with short stories and several illustrations.

The Society of Ukrainian Philatelists, Inc., of New York City, started to publish Ukrainskyi Filatelist (The Ukrainian Philatelist), a publication which sheds light on Ukrainian stamps, individual collections, medals, and other related topics.

1952    November 1 - 8. At the 29th Annual Women's International Exhibit organized in New York City, the Ukrainian Committee participated with an interesting folk art exhibit, and presented Ukrainian songs and dances.

The Ukrainian Museum-Archive was established in Cleveland, Ohio, as a center of collecting Ukrainian heritage objects and publications. It has also been very active in publishing Ukrainian postage stamps.

The Ukrainian Artist's Association in the United States came into existence and encompassed more than 100 painters, sculptors, and graphic artists. It staged several art exhibits in different cities. Michael Moroz, Edward Kozak, Jaques Hnizdovsky, Michael Chereshniovsky, Nicholas Mukhyn became leading names in American artistic circles, and their works became very popular with art lovers. The Association organized evening courses in painting, graphic arts and sculpture.

Nick Adams (born Adamschock), a leading movie actor, made his debut in the film Somebody Loves Me. He appeared later in several other movies and usually played neurotic and agressive types.

1953    April 10 - 12. The Federation of Ukrainian Student Organizations of America (SUSTA) was founded in New York City as a body uniting Ukrainian American student organizations in colleges, universities, as well as student clubs, religious, cultural or sport groups. Its main scope has been to encourage the study of Ukrainian culture, and it has played a very active role in the establishing of a Ukrainian chair at Harvard University.

The Ukrainian Chorus Dumka of New York City initiated the formation of a Ukrainian symphony orchestra.

October. The Association of Former Ukrainian Political Prisoners was founded in New York City, concentrating all former inmates who suffered at the hands of Soviet, Polish or German Fascist authorities because of their belief in and fight for an independent Ukraine.

Vilna Ukraina (Free Ukraine) was started as a political quarterly by the Ukrainian Free Society of America, a leftist group supporting Ukrainian socialist ideology. The publication covers Ukrainian history, politics, and social aspects.

1954        The Ukrainian Life Cooperative Association was created in Chicago, Illinois, to disseminate information to Ukrainian Americans who do not read English. It has only about 150 members.

The Holy Ukrainian Autocephalous Orthodox Church in Exile was founded by a group of post World War II Ukrainian immigrants, and it presently has about 5,000 members. Its official organ is Pravoslavnyi Ukrainets (The Orthodox Ukrainian), a quarterly concerned with church organization and religious education.

Nicholas Sydor-Czartorysky of New York City started publishing Biblos, a quarterly bibliographic trade magazine, containing bibliographic listings and short book reviews.

Likarskyi Visnyk Zhurnal Ukrainskoho Likarskoho Tovarystva Pivnichnoi Ameryky (Journal of the Ukrainian Medical Association of North America) started publication as a quarterly devoted to medical papers in Ukrainian and to medical terminology.

The Ukrainian National Association started publishing Veselka (The Rainbow), an illustrated monthly magazine destined for pre-school and school-age children, aiming at cultivating and preserving the Ukrainian spiritual heritage.

Dr. Wasyl Luciw of State College, Pennsylvania, started Zhyttia I Shkola (Life and School), a bi-monthly publishing reprints of older Ukrainian articles on Ukrainian culture, history, bibliography, as well as some new articles on the same subjects.

Mykola Yelychevsky of Irvington, New Jersey, started publishing Ukrainskyi Hospodarnyk (The Ukrainian Economist), a journal of Ukrainian economists in the United States, devoted to the history of the Ukrainian economy and trends in the development of Ukrainian economy.

Tania Kroitor Bishop (born Shevchuk) of Spokane, Washington, poet and translator, published An Overture to Future Days, a volume of poetry in English and Ukrainian. She later rendered other translations from Ukrain-

ian into English and made contributions to several
magazines.

1955       January 21 - 23.  Governor Averell Harriman of New
York State and Mayor Robert Wagner of New York City
proclaimed the days of January 21 and 23 as Ukrainian
days in New York State and New York City.

June 28.  Representatives of Ukrainian American organizations participated in the National Unity Day held in
New York City, featuring Ukrainian national costumes
and Ukrainian national flags.

The Ukrainian Lawyer's Organization in the United
States started publishing Pravnychnyi Visnyk (The
Law Journal), containing articles on Ukrainian law,
history, and book reviews as well as bibliographies.

The Ukrainian Life Cooperative Association started the
publication of Ukrainske Zhyttia (Ukrainian Life),
an independent weekly shedding light on political,
cultural, and social events in the Ukraine, and other
countries.

John Hodiak died at the age of forty-one in Hollywood,
California, leaving behind a career of a leading movie
actor.

1956       The Union of Ukrainian American Sport Clubs was founded.
Its members were mostly post World War II Ukrainian
immigrants.

Zenon Snylyk, a leading Ukrainian American soccer star,
played with the United States Olympic soccer team.

The Ukrainian American community of New York City commemorated fifty years of organized life under the auspices of the Ukrainian American Organization Committee
of New York City.  A Golden Jubillee Book devoted to
this event was edited by Dr. Aleksander Sokolyshyn, a
noted researcher and bibliographer on Ukrainian subjects

Myroslow Prokop started the publication of Digest of
the Ukrainian Press, a monthly translating articles
from the Soviet Ukrainian press.

Two Carpatho-Ukrainian Catholic units, the Munhall
Archdiocese of Pittsburgh, Pennsylvania, and the Passayc
New Jersey Eparchy, started publishing Byzantine Catholic World, and respectively Eastern Catholic Life, two
weeklies featuring religious news of interest to Catholic parishioners.

1957          Sandra Dee (born Alexandra Zhuk), a former model, made
              her debut as movie actress in the film Until They Sail
              followed by The Reluctant Debutante.  She later suc-
              cessfully appeared in several other movies during the
              sixties.

              The Ukrainian Brotherhood of Metropolitan Vasil
              Lypkivsky of Chicago, Illinois, started publishing
              Tserkva I Zhyttia (Church and Life), a bi-monthly sup-
              porting the position of the Ukrainian Orthodox Auto-
              cephalous Church.

              The Association for the Liberation of the Ukraine
              started publishing Missiia Ukrainy (Mission of Ukraine),
              devoted to political, cultural, and social events in
              the Ukraine, as well as organizational news.

              The Ukrainian Archive-Museum was established in Detroit,
              Michigan.

1958          The Selfreliance Association of American Ukrainians
              started to publish Nash Svit (Our World) mainly con-
              cerned with Ukrainian economic life in the United
              States.

              The Ukrainian National Museum was founded in Chicago,
              Illinois, by the merger of the former Ukrainian Nation-
              al Museum and Library of Ontario, Canada, and the Ukrain-
              ian Archive-Museum of Chicago, Illinois.

1959          President Dwight D. Eisenhower named Professor George
              Kistiakowsky as his Special Assistant for Science and
              Technology.  Professor Kistiakowsky, a member of the
              National Academy of Science, published more than 150
              scientific articles in different professional journals.

              The United Societies of the U.S.A., a Carpatho-Ukrainian
              organization also known under the name of Sobranie,
              started publishing Prosvita (Enlightenment), devoted to
              fraternal benefit interests and to religious news.

              The New York Group, a circle of young poets including
              Bohdan Boychuk, Zhenia Vasylivska, Patricia Kylyna,
              Yurii Tarnavsky, and others, published its first volume
              of modern poetry and started a path of new trends in
              Ukrainian literature.

1960          Professor Lev Dobriansky, a prominent Ukrainian Ameri-
              can leader and scholar, published his book Decisions
              for a Better America.  He is also the author and co-
              author of several other books and presently the head
              of the Ukrainian Congress Committee of America.

The Ukrainian Nationals-Trident, a soccer club of
Philadelphia, Pennsylvania, won the United States
soccer championship.

The Ukrainian School Societies of Chicago, Illinois,
started publishing Ekran Illustrovannyi Dvo-Misiachnyk
Ukrainskoho Zhyttia, an illustrated magazine covering
historical, cultural, religious, and political events
regarding the Ukrainians in America and in other countries.

The Ukrainian National Union of New York City started
publishing Tryzub (Trident), a bi-monthly concerned
with Ukrainian history and political life. The trident,
a three-pronged spear, has been the Ukrainian national
emblem since early times.

Joseph Charyk, president of the Communication Satelite
Corporation, was appointed Air Force undersecretary and
served in this capacity for three years.

1961        The Ukrainian Research and Information Institute was
            established in Chicago, Illinois, to conduct research
            in the socio-economic and political fields of the
            Ukraine. The institute is supported by about 300 his-
            torians, economists, educators and scientists.

            L. Lyman of New York City started publishing Notatnyk
            (Diary), a monthly devoted to events in the Ukraine
            and other countries.

            Terry Sawchuk was elected to the Hockey Hall of Fame
            and is considered one of the greatest goalies in his-
            tory. He finished his championship with 103 shootouts,
            the only goalie ever to reach the century mark.

1962        The Ukrainian Librarian's Association of America
            started issuing Biuleten (Bulletin), a publication
            containing bibliographical notes, brief articles, and
            news regarding the activities of the association.

            Sydir Krawec of New York City published Nasha Batkiv-
            shchyna (Our Fatherland), a bi-monthly carrying general
            and local news of interest to the Ukrainians of Ortho-
            dox faith, as well as articles on Ukrainian history,
            culture, political and religious life. It is still in
            existence.

            The Institute of Ukrainian Culture of Detroit, Michigan,
            began publishing Terem.Problemy Ukrainskoii Kultury,
            Neperiodychnyi Iliustrovanyi Zhurnal (Terem.Problems
            of Ukrainian Culture), with the purpose of gathering
            information on the status and growth of Ukrainian cul-

ture in the free world.

The John the Baptist Ukrainian Catholic Church was
completed in Hunter, New York. The church is a fine
example of ancient Ukrainian wooden church architecture, popular in Carpatho-Ukraine.

Mike Souchak, a prominent golf player, officially won
194,734.11 dollars after a decade of important vic-
tories. Another noted golf player was Steve Melnik.

1963          The Karpaty Publishers of New York City started issuing Holos Lemkivshchyny (The Lemko Voice), a monthly
concerned with Lemko Ukrainians in America, Poland,
and the Ukraine. It also provided local and general
news.

The Ukrainian American Youth Association began publishing Krylati (The Winged Ones), a monthly magazine destined for young readers and covering Ukrainian history
and culture, as well as current events in Ukrainian
American life.

The Ukrainian Artist's Association in U.S.A. started
to put out Notatky Z Mystectva (Ukrainian Art Digest),
a publication shedding light on Ukrainian artists and
their works.

The Ukrainian Genealogical and Heraldic Society of
Miami Shores, Florida, started to publish a Bulletin
covering organizational and activity news of the society.

The Ukrainian Historical Society was founded and began
publishing Ukrainskyi Istoryk (The Ukrainian Historian),
a quarterly devoted to Ukrainian and East European political, social, and cultural history.

The Ukrainian Research and Information Institute published Za Pravdu Pro Ukrainu (For the Truth About
Ukraine), a bulletin tending to correct major historical and political misconceptions regarding the Ukraine
and the Ukrainians as described in the English publications. The publication is still in existence, but
appears irregularly.

Jack Palance, noted movie actor, appeared in the television series entitled The Greatest Show on Earth. He
previously distinguished himself in the movie Requiem
for a Heavyweight, and won a Sylvania Award.

Marie Halun-Bloch, an authoress of children's books,
published Aunt America, a fine patriotic narration

that won high commendation from critics and readers
alike. Marie Halun-Bloch also published Ukrainian
folk tales and several other books.

1964          February 25. The sculptor Alexander Archipenko died
              at the age of seventy-seven in New York City. Shortly
              before he died, Archipenko had his 119th one-man art
              exhibition. His works can be found in all major art
              museums of the world.

              June 27. Former President Dwight D. Eisenhower unveiled
              a statue of Taras Shevchenko, the great Ukrainian poet,
              in Washington, D. C., at a ceremony which attracted more
              than 100,000 Ukrainians from the United States, Canada,
              and other countries. Ukrainians were celebrating the
              150th anniversary of the poet's birth. (See 1814)

              Zenon Snylyk again played with the United States
              Olympic Soccer Team. He also was a member of the
              United States World Cup Team and represented our
              country in fifty-one international matches.

              The Ukrainian Nationals, a soccer team of Philadelphia,
              Pennsylvania, won the United States Soccer Championship.

1965          Reverend Jaroslav Swyschuk of Chicago, Illinois, started
              publishing Nova Zorya (New Star), a Catholic weekly de-
              voted to Ukrainian education, religion, and culture.

              The Ukrainian Sports Club of New York City won the
              United States Soccer Championship.

              The New York Ukrainians, a New York City soccer team,
              took away the title of United States Soccer Champion
              from the Ukrainian Nationals of Philadelphia, Pennsyl-
              vania, but for only one year.

1967          The Hutsul Association of Chicago, Illinois, started
              publishing Hutsuliya, a quarterly dealing with the
              Ukrainian Hutsul group, their land, history, and culture.

              The Ukrainian Historical Association put out a Bulletin
              reflecting organizational news and the status of Ukrain-
              ian scholarship in the United States and other coun-
              tries.

              The Ukrainian Journalist's Association of America pub-
              lished Ukrainskyi Zhurnalist (The Ukrainian Journalist),
              a bulletin covering specifically journalism events and
              news.

              Stephan Procych of Philadelphia, Pennsylvania, started
              a publication called Za Patriarchat (For the Patriar-

chate), a quarterly advocating the establishment of a
Ukrainian Catholic patriarchate in the United States.

The Ukrainian Workingmen's Association started publishing Forum: A Ukrainian Review, a quarterly devoted to
the Ukraine, Ukrainian Americans, and Ukrainian communities from other countries, destined for high school
and college students.

Charles Bednarick was elected to the Football Hall of
Fame.

November 12 - 19. The first World Congress of Free
Ukrainians took place in New York City, and attracted
representatives from Ukrainian communities from all
over the world.

Bohdan Wynar, a library science professor and author
of several books on cataloging, bibliography, and
reference, established a new publishing house, Libraries Unlimited, mainly for reference books of interest
to schools and university libraries.

1968     January 22. The Harvard Ukrainian Studies Center was
established at Harvard University as a result of financial and moral support received from large numbers of
Ukrainian Americans. The center is headed by Dr.
Omeljan Pritsak, a prominent Ukrainian American orient-
alist, and offers courses in Ukrainian language, literature
and history leading to doctoral degrees in Ukrainian
studies. It also publishes scholarly works, textbooks
and reprints.

The Saints Volodymyr and Olha Ukrainian Catholic Parish
of Chicago, Illinois, started publishing Cerkovnyj
Visnyk (The Church Herald), a bi-monthly concerned
with Ukrainian Catholic life and the Ukrainian cultural
heritage.

The Ukrainian Free Cossaks Brotherhood of Chicago,
Illinois, started issuing Ukrainske Kozatstvo (The
Ukrainian Cossakdom), a quarterly of Ukrainian veterans devoted to Cossak traditions, history, and present
activities.

Dr. Walter Tkach became President Richard Nixon's phy-
sician. Dr. Tkach previously served as assistant phy-
sician to President Dwight D. Eisenhower, and later
spent three years in Vietnam as the commanding surgeon
of the Seventh Air Force Division.

Movie actor Nick Adams died at the age of thirty-seven.
A few years before his death, Adams appeared in the

television series <u>Johnny</u> <u>Yuma</u>.

Dr. Michael Yarymovich was appointed deputy assistant to the Air Force secretary for research and development.

1969     The Boykivshchyna Association of Philadelphia, Pennsylvania, started publishing <u>Litopys Boykivshchyna</u> (Journal Boykivshchyna), a quarterly devoted to the study of the Ukrainians who came from the region of Boykiv, their history, and language.

The New York City Ukrainian Student Hromada started publishing <u>Novi Napriamy</u> (New Directions), a bi-monthly providing space for a free student discussion on contemporary problems facing the Ukrainian American community.

The Ukrainian Genealogical and Heraldic Society put out <u>Zapysky</u> (Memoirs), a bi-monthly dealing with Ukrainian genealogy, heraldry, and other topics.

The Ukrainian National Association sponsored an original Ukrainian opera called <u>Yaroslavna</u>, based on an historic subject. The music was composed by Anton Rudnitsky, and the lyrics were written by Leonid Poltava.

1970     The Ukrainian Academy of Arts and Sciences in the United States started publishing <u>Visti Uvan</u> (News of Academy), reflecting the academy's activities, as well as short biographies, bibliographies, and other news.

<u>Recenzija</u> (A Review), a semi-annual publication dealing with critical reviews of Ukrainian scholarly materials published in the Soviet Ukraine, was started by Ukrainian students at Harvard University in Boston, Massachusetts.

The Federation of Ukrainian Students Organizations of Michnovsky, Detroit Branch, started publishing <u>Soniashnyk</u> (Sunflower), a quarterly covering political and cultural aspects of the Ukrainian Americans.

Walter Tkaczuk and Dave Balon, both players for the New York Rangers, were members of the National Hockey League's highest scoring line during the 1969-1970 season.

1971     Roman Kupchynsky of New York City started a monthly publication <u>Kryza</u> (The Crisis), advocating the creation of a Ukrainian Catholic patriarchate in the United States.

The Shevchenko Scientific Society of New York City,
in cooperation with the Ukrainian Library Association,
started issuing Ukrainska Knyha (The Ukrainian Book),
a bibliographical quarterly covering literature, history, and other topics.

Lemkovina (Lemko Land), a monthly publication dealing
with political, social, and other aspects of the Lemko
Ukrainians in the United States, Poland, and the Ukraine,
was started by the Lemkovina Press of Yonkers, New York.

Johnny Bucyk, a prominent player for the Boston Bruins,
was selected for the National Hockey League's 1971 All-
Star team.  Bucyk, together with Vic Stasiuk and Bronko
Horvath, formed the famous "Uke" line in our national
hockey during the fifties.

1973      June.  Cardinal Joseph Slipyi arrived in New York City,
and received a very warm reception from Ukrainian
Catholics.  Cardinal Slipyi is a prominent leader and
fighter for a Ukrainian Catholic patriarchate in the
United States, but his views are not accepted by the
Vatican.

1974      The Ukrainian National Women's League of America presented a collection of books on Ukrainian Americans to
the American Museum of Immigration at the Statue of
Liberty in New York City.

Ukrainian publishers, bookstore owners and librarians
from the United States and Canada established a Ukrainian bookstore center with the purpose of fostering the
development of Ukrainian publications, popularizing
and disseminating Ukrainian books in the free world.

June 29 and 30 were declared "Ukrainian Pioneers Days"
in North Dakota in honor of the first Ukrainian American settlers in this state.  (See 1890)

1975      January.  An exhibition with paintings by Taras Shu-
milovich of New York City was opened in the building
of the Providential Savings Bank in New York City.

February.  The Bronx Society of Engineers celebrated
George Golovchenko for his outstanding professional
activities, and contributions to the development of
the society during several decades.

April.  Dr. Michael Yarymovich of College Park, Maryland, was appointed Assistant Administrator for Laboratory and Field Coordination of the Energy Research
and development Administration.  Dr. Yarymovich is
a prominent scientist who served as assistant direct-
or to the Apollo Flight Systems.  (See 1968)

DOCUMENTS

# THE FIRST UKRAINIAN DAY PROCLAIMED IN THE UNITED STATES 1917

On March 2, 1917, the United States Senate and House of Representatives voted Joint Resolution 201 and requested the President of the United States to designate a day for the relief of stricken Ukrainians from the belligerent countries of Eastern Europe. President Woodrow Wilson approved the resolution, and proclaimed April 21, 1917 as Ukrainian Day. Here are the remarks made by Congressman James Hamill, whose arguments played the most important role in passing the documents favorable to the Ukrainian cause.

Source: U. S. Statutes at Large, 64th Congress (1915-1917), vol. 39, part 1, and Appendix to the Congressional Record, 64th Congress, 2nd session.

## The Ruthenians (Ukrainians).

---

## EXTENSION OF REMARKS
OF
# HON. JAMES A. HAMILL,
OF NEW JERSEY,

## IN THE HOUSE OF REPRESENTATIVES,
*Wednesday, February 21, 1917.*

On Senate joint resolution (S. J. Res. 201) requesting the President to appoint a day for the relief of the Ruthenians (Ukrainians).

Mr. HAMILL. Mr. Speaker, this resolution was conceived in a spirit of humanity. It explains its own purpose. Millions of Ruthenians have been sorely oppressed and scourged by the ravages of war in eastern Europe, and no helping hand has thus far been extended to them, save the feeble assistance which a few of their own people from the Ukrain now residing in America have been able to render.

The matter was first brought to my attention by the very reverend administrator of the Ruthenian Catholic Diocese in the United States, the Rev. Father P. Poniatishin, through his counsel, Mr. William J. Kearns, of the New Jersey bar. Before the Christmas holidays Mr. Kearns consulted me with reference to the adoption of some measure of relief for the Ukrainians, especially for those in war-stricken Galicia, Bukowina, and other Provinces of Austria. Then I received a letter from the very reverend administrator, which I beg to insert, as follows:

NEWARK, N. J., *December 27, 1916.*

Hon. JAMES A. HAMILL, M. C.,
                    *Jersey City, N. J.*

MY DEAR CONGRESSMAN: I have to thank you most cordially for
the deep interest you are taking in the cause of our Ruthenian war
sufferers, and to say that the Ruthenians who have made their homes
in this country will always feel that they owe you a sincere debt of
gratitude. In our diocese in the United States there are at least
600,000 souls from Galicia, besides some 500,000 more Ruthenians, who
are also of Ukrainian origin, from Hungary, Bukowina, and other parts
of Austria. I know I speak the true sentiment of my people in ex-
pressing our warmest appreciation of your efforts in their behalf.
These people deeply sympathize with their afflicted brothers, but have
been unable to render them much practical assistance in their great
misfortunes and terrible sufferings. Millions of our people in Galicia
have been deprived of all their property and belongings and are in
actual need of the necessaries of life. In Galicia alone, prior to the
war, there was a Ruthenian population of some 4,000,000. At least
1,000,000 of these former inhabitants have been driven out of their
country through the scourge of war, and are wandering without home
or friends through other parts of the Austrian Empire. These Ukrainians seem to have been forgotten, or overlooked, for notwithstanding
that measures of relief have been undertaken for other nationalities,
nothing whatever of a systematic, regular character has yet been done
for them. If the President of the United States would designate a
day for the collection of funds to relieve their destitution I feel that
America out of its great, generous heart would respond nobly. May I,
therefore, supplement the request of my counsel, Mr. Kearns, that you
stand sponsor for a resolution requesting the President so to act?
    With sentiments of deep respect, I am,
        Very sincerely, yours,
                            P. PONIATISHIN, *Administrator.*

On January 3, 1917, Very Rev. P. Poniatishin, with his
counsel, came to Washington with reference to this measure and
enlisted my interest more thoroughly. On January 23, 1917,
they visited the Capitol again, and on January 24, 1917, the
resolution was introduced in this House and simultaneously
in the Senate. Senator HUGHES of New Jersey stood sponsor
for it in the other House, and the Senate Committee on Foreign
Relations reported it with unanimous approval. It passed the
Senate and has now been substituted on the House calendar
for my measure. It appeals to the humanitarian instinct of
every Member of this House. It breathes the spirit of a broad
charity. The great American heart will unquestionably respond
with a warm and generous sympathy, and prompt the citizens
of our country, irrespective of racial origin, to aid materially
millions of their fellow human beings whose sufferings are
simply incredible and who are unable to help themselves.

    Probably no section in all war-stricken Europe has undergone
so terrible an affliction as has the country inhabited by the
Ruthenians in eastern Galicia and the northwestern part of
Bukowina. Before the war, in Galicia alone there dwelt
4,000,000 of these people. Their country has been so terribly
ravaged by war that it may be regarded as almost irretrievably
ruined, for its people are scattered and hundreds of thousands
of them are to-day homeless and lack the very necessaries of
life. College professors, clergymen, lawyers, doctors, and merchants have been deprived of their all and their families reduced
to destitution, and compelled actually to beg for bread. They
lack necessary clothing to protect them against the cold of an
Austrian winter, and many of them, according to reliable reports, are absolutely without shoes and stockings. Their country has been overrun and raked fore and aft by the most terrible war ever known, not only three or four times in general
military movements, but by innumerable deadly and devastat-
ing minor skirmishes, entailing vast suffering and destitution.
Since the taking of Lemberg and its recapture, and both prior
to and since the siege and fall of Przemysl, there has been an
uninterrupted, desolating warfare raging throughout this region,
which has told most terribly upon the Ruthenian population.

    No contributions or measures of relief collected or intended
for the other war sufferers ever reach these Ruthenians.
Theirs is a typical instance of a people who have been actually
submerged; they are, in fact, a forgotten race, and yet these
Ukrainians constitute a nation just as clearly and sharply defined as do the Poles, the Russians, or the Bulgarians. There

are few people who understand that the Russian tongue is a language as foreign to a Ruthenian as French is to an Italian. Unfortunately these people and their country are little known either in Europe or America, although they have existed for centuries as a distinct race and nation, while their ancient capital of Kiev, on the river Dneiper, rivaled at one time in wealth and magnificence the capital of the Eastern Roman Empire, but that was before it was pillaged and destroyed by the Muscovites.

The Ukraine covers about 328,185 square miles, and its territory is therefore one and one-half times as large as the present-day Germany. In eastern Galicia, the northwest of Bukowina, and the northeast of Hungary there is a Ruthenian population of 4,200,000 souls, or rather there was such a population there before the war began, while the Ruthenian race, populating the Ukraine, numbers, or rather did number prior to the war, nearly 40,000,000 souls. Millions of them have been slain, maimed, crippled, and irreparably ruined by the belligerents on both sides, and no hand has been raised as yet in any regular or systematic way to relieve the distress of this particular people.

The first Ukrainian immigrants came to America about 40 years ago. Many of them came here to better their economic conditions; some of them fled before the political and religious persecution. This tide of immigration has immensely increased in late years, and continued until the war began. At present there are a million Ukrainians in the United States, and 200,000 in Canada. In Canada they are mostly farmers, having settled in the great wheat-producing Provinces of Manitoba, Saskatchewan, and Alberta. In the United States they are laborers, miners, farmers, skilled workmen, and business men. The conditions in America from the very beginning favored the development of the Ukrainian immigrant. The man that under the oppressive circumstances in the old country seemed doomed to eternal dependence had here in America a chance. As it is usually the case with all the Slavonic immigrants, the Ukrainians settled in large colonies in different industrial centers. Having provided homes for their families, their next endeavor was to provide for their own spiritual needs, and on this they never spare money and sacrifice. So the churches were built, beneficial and educational organizations were founded, economical, cooperative institutions were started, and many Ukrainian papers founded. The Ukrainians are very much interested in all these institutions, and it is considered as a national duty to be the member of at least one of them. Usually at the churches parochial schools are organized, for the purpose of teaching the children the Ukrainian language as well as the principles upon which the American civilization is built. The Ukrainians have a full confidence in the American schools, and are eager to send their children there.

#### CONCLUSION.

Now, however, that the terrible plight of these people, who were almost a forgotten race, has been brought to the attention of the American Congress, and that the American President has raised his voice in behalf of the submerged peoples of the world, a glimmer of hope has even come to the Ruthenians, who were well-nigh on the brink of despair—in fact, who were actually in despair—of their receiving some temporary provisional relief. Therefore, may they hopefully look forward to some amelioration of their present condition of misery and wretchedness. Hence, Mr. Speaker, I bespeak for this resolution the unanimous vote of the House. In this appeal I am joined by my colleague, Mr. FARR, of Pennsylvania, who has enthusiastically supported and aided me in all my endeavors to have this resolution enacted.

SURVEY OF UKRAINIAN AMERICANS
1919

The following is the first brief survey on
Ukrainian and Canadian Americans, prepared
as a lesson in patriotism, and especially designed for school use.

Source:  Literary Digest, (November 15, 1919).

UKRAINIANS IN AMERICA

A LARGE ELEMENT OF THE POPULATION -- Among European countries that entered on a new era of existence through the dissolutions of the
World War is Ukraine; and of its nationals more than 1,000,000, approximately, are inhabitants of the United States. Most of them have come from
East Galicia, the part of Ukraine formerly subject to the late Austro-Hungarian Empire. Only about 15% of the total number of Ukrainians in this
country are from Western Russian Ukraine. The principal distinction between the two kinds of Ukrainians lies in religious affiliation and educational
advancement. The Ukrainians from East Galicia are Greek Catholics; those
from the Russian Ukraine are members of the Russian Orthodox Church.
The latter, under the Czarist regime, were held in thrall to the Russian
language, ideas and education. They were practically all of the peasant class.
The Austrian Government was more liberal with the result that East Galicia became the seat of Ukrainian culture.
        WHERE THEY ARE SETTLED -- The largest proportion of our Ukrain-
ian population is settled in the Eastern and Middle Western sections of the
country. They are most thickly congregated in Pennsylvania, New York,
the lower New England States, in Ohio, Michigan, Illinois, and Missouri.
As farmers they are fairly numerous in North Dakota and Minnesota. There
are small agricultural colonies of Ukrainians in California, and in Oregon,
some colonies employed in the lumber industry. In the Eastern and Middle
Western States the Ukrainians are employed in steel mills, coal and iron
mines. They are mostly factory workers in the New England States. It is
to be noted, moreover, that in the greater towns and cities many Ukrainians
are carpenters, cabinet makers and furriers. . Also in the big cities not a
few are workers in hotels and restaurants. Some also are shopkeepers and
tradesmen. They have co-operative stores in Connecticut and in Pennsylvania. There are more Ukrainians in the Keystone State than in any other.
In one town a Ukrainian bank, established two years ago,  holds today
$1,000,000 in deposits. In another, Northampton, there is a population of
12,000 of which about 70% is Ukrainian. They work in cement mills. Among
cities New York is credited with the two largest Ukrainian colonies, one of
which is settled on the East Side from Second to Sixth Street and the other

also on the East Side, but in the vicinity of 72nd Street. In the latter neigh-
borhood there is also a colony of Czecho-Slovaks. Ukrainians are to be met
in considerable number also in Williamsburg and the Bronx, in Greater New
York, and in Jersey City and Newark, New Jersey. There is a notable Ukrainian population in Scranton and in Harrisburg, Pa., while in Pittsburg and its
environs the Ukrainian population is estimated at 80,000.

TIDAL FLOW OF IMMIGRATION -- About twenty years ago the Ukrainians began to come to this country in great numbers, which increased until
they were landing here at the estimated rate of 100,000 per year. The outbreak of war in 1914 resulted in the stoppage of their immigration. The
great majority of the Ukrainian immigrants were men, ranging from early
manhood to the forties. Ukrainian women immigrants usually entered domestic service or became workers in hotels and textile mills. Because of
the great number of Ukrainian men here their opportunity of marriage was
at hand and as soon as they were married they settled down to the career
of homemaking - as the mothers of American homes. Their children receive their education in our public schools and it happens more often than
not, especially in larger centres, that these children of Ukrainian descent
grow up with only a fractional knowledge of the Ukrainian tongue. The
Ukrainians maintain private schools in some sections where the language
and literature of Ukraine are taught in night classes. These born American
citizens naturally abide in this country. In the American forces during the
war there were 30,000 men of Ukrainian descent. As an extremely thrifty
and prosperous race, in whatever calling, the Ukrainians were among the
heaviest buyers of Liberty Bonds in the class of foreign nationals. Also the
Ukrainians were the only foreign nation which insisted that the purchaser
of bonds must make a cash payment at the time of purchase.

SOCIAL ORGANIZATION OF THE UKRAINIANS -- Among notable organizations of the Ukrainians are their gymnastic societies called "Sich",
of which there are 300 branches in the United States. Then there are many
benevolent societies, of which the foremost is the Ukrainian National Association, with headquarters in Jersey City. It has 500 branches. In Philadelphia is the headquarters of another benevolent society which has 200 branches.
Religiously considered in the United States the great mass of Ukrainians
are Greek Catholics, and have more than 100 churches here. Some Ukrainians have become Protestants in this country and are mainly affiliated with
the Presbyterian denomination. They have seven churches variously distrib-
uted. There are about a dozen Ukrainian newspapers which are mostly of
tri-weekly issue. Their chief social and educational medium is the Ukrainian National Committee, whose purpose is to instruct the Ukrainians in the
ideals, institutions and history of the United States, while it also keeps them
informed about the conditions and progress of the land of their forebears.
This organization, founded on Armistice Day, is a patriotic outgrowth of the
Liberty Loan Campaigns and it has 180 local chapters which represent more
than 1,000 local societies.

UKRAINIANS IN CANADA -- In Canada there are 500,000 Ukrainians who are prosperous farmers in Saskatchewan, Manitoba and Alberta. Whole sections in these provinces are so thoroughly Ukrainian that the Canadian Government has provided bi-lingual schools. The Ukrainians have more than 200 churches here and one priest in some cases conducts the services in several churches. There are about 10 Ukrainian newspapers in Canada. In Winnipeg, Manitoba, there are about 40,000 Ukrainians who live mainly in one district that is regarded as the Ukrainian district. In the large Eastern cities, , as for instance Montreal and Toronto, there is a limited Ukrainian population. In the Canadian overseas forces there were 20,000 Ukrainians. A curious instance of intimacy between nations, which became such an every-day matter among the Allies, is found in the Canadian bi-lingual schools in Ukrainian districts. Here the Canadian boys and girls learn with their lessons the folk songs of Ukraine, which are described as being of great variety and beauty.

# THE UKRAINIAN IMMIGRANTS
# IN THE UNITED STATES
# 1940

Yaroslav J. Chyz, a noted scholar on
Ukrainian Americans, published a very
interesting comprehensive study on
Ukrainian Americans. The study is entirely reproduced below.

Source: Chyz, Yaroslav J. The Ukrain-
ian Immigrants in the United States.
Scranton, Pennsylvania: The Ukrainian
Workingmen's Association, 1940 (reprint).

Immigrants from Ukrainian territories in Europe have been listed in the United States under various names. American writers and encyclopedias used the names "Little Russians" and "Ruthenians," following the Russian and Austrian official appellations. The United States immigration authorities use the names "Ruthenians" and "Russniaks," and the United States Census listed them first as Ruthenians and lately (in 1930) as Ukrainians and Ruthenians. Some of the Ukrainian immigrants call themselves Carpatho-Russians or Russians to indicate their preference for Russian culture or their desire to see Ukrainian territories in Europe under Russian rule. Local names, such as "Roosin" and "Lemko," denoting immigrants from Carpatho-Ukraine or from the westernmost part of the Ukrainian territory, are also in use.

The name "Ukrainian" is now prevalent among the Ukrainians themselves and in the American press and political literature. It is applied to immigrants from Soviet Ukraine and Ukrainian territories of Soviet Russia, from Western (now also Soviet) Ukraine, from Rumanian provinces of Bukovina and Bessarabia, from Carpatho-Ukraine (now under Hungarian rule) and from Lemkivschina, now under German and Slovak occupation. [1]

In this article the name "Ukrainian" is applied to the whole Ukrainian group in the United States. The terms "Ruthenian," "Russian" (in reference to a Ukrainian group) and "Carpatho-Russian" are used only in cases where the name, by which a particular group prefers to be known, is quoted.

### Early Ukrainian Arrivals

Although Ukrainians could have learned about the New World from the writings of Joannes Glogoviensis [2] and Jan Stobnica [3] of the University of

1. For distribution of Ukrainian population in Europe, see following: Elisee Reclus, **Universal Geography**, Vol. 5, London, 1878-94; Stephen Rudnitsky, **Ukraine, the Land and Its People**, Rand, McNally & Co., New York, 1918; Henri F. Klein, "Ukraine" in **Encyclopedia Americana**, Vol. XXVII, New York-Chicago, 1932.
2. Avrahm Yarmolinsky, "Introductorium Compendiosum by John of Glogau," **Bulletin of the New York Public Library**, Vol. 37, 8, 1933.
3. Same author, "Stobnica's Introductio in Ptolomei Cosmographiam," **Bulletin of the New York Public Library**, Vol. 38, 4, 1934.

Cracow, or from manuscripts of the holy monk Maxim Grek [4] as early as the first half of the sixteenth century, there are no traces of any intercourse between America and Ukraine until one hundred years later. At that time the second Governor of Virginia, John Smith, of Pocahontas fame, while escaping from Turkish captivity, passed through Ukraine and left an interesting page in his memoirs, describing his journey from Richycia, on the Dnipro river, to Kolomea, at the foot of the Carpathian Mountains. [5]

Later on various records of early American history yield a few names, which might have belonged to newcomers from Ukraine. The pitch maker, Molasco, one of the "Polonians" brought by the same John Smith to Virginia to "make pitch and tarr and sope ashes," [6] could have been a Ukrainian or White Russian. His name does not sound Polish and Poland at that time was in three fourths populated by Ukrainians, White Russians and Lithuanians.

Also, the founder of the family of Zabriskie, who in 1662 arrived in New York under the name of Albert Saboriski, was probably a Ukrainian exile from Poland. His only known signature on a sale document of July 15, 1679, reads: "Albridt Zaborowskij." All other transcriptions of his name always contain the letter "i" instead of the second "o" (Saborsiski, Zaborisco, Zaborisko, Zaborischo, Zabrowisky, Zabborwisco, Zaboriskwy, Saborisky, Zabbroisco, Zaborischoo), which is a very characteristic mark of the Ukrainian language. It is, therefore, possible that he signed his name the way he was taught in Polish-Latin schools — "Zaborowsky," but pronounced it "Zaboriwsky" in Ukrainian. This resulted in the many above variations of his name, as it was written down by others. [7]

About the same time the records, of what was then New Amsterdam, mention another name that has a Ukrainian sound — Marcus Duschosche (Dushkowsky). In Pennsylvania among the immigrants, who arrived between 1726-1776, are such Ukrainian-sounding names

4. Same author, "Studies in Russian Americana," Bulletin of the New York Library, Vol. 43, 7, 1939.

5. Travels and Works of Captain John Smith, president of Virginia and Admiral of New England, 1580-1631. Edited by Edward Arber F. S. A., New Edition, Edinburgh, John Grant, 1910.

6. The Records of the Virginia Company of London. The Court Book. Edited by Susan Myra Kingsbury, Washington, 1906.

7. Rychard Wynkoop, Zabriskie Notes, The New York Genealogical and Biographical Record,. Vol. XXIII, New York, 1893.

as Nicholas Orich, Peter Looh, Daniel Zwier, Martin Blisky, Johan Peter Lach, Christian Wenger, Anthony Samber, Elias Stocki, Jacob Sheyco, Andreas Kissel, Johannes Hirni, Christian Closs, Jacob Shable, Peter Step, Albertus Roosin, Matheis Hora, Geo. Michael Vuss, Martin Rudy, Chistian Hallitchke, Anna Kunegunda Russ and many others. [8] Of course, there is no proof that they were Ukrainians, but their names certainly read like a register of some Ukrainian society of today.

The same can be said about the lists of soldiers in the American Revolutionary Army. In the State of Pennsylvania alone among its soldiers the following are named: Jacob Knias (also Kunias), Henry Donich, Dennis Bohan, Nicholas Beesun, Peter Polin, Stephen Cisna, William Eavan, Christofer Chisar, John Moch, Stephen Soobley (also Zoobley), Isaak Follis, Thomas Chesney, John Ottaman, Conrad Carrass, Andrew Caravin, David Latta, and many others with names popular among Ukrainians. [9] The Revo-

lutionary navy bought is supplies from Samuel Hrabowski in Charleston, S. C.; Thomas Masney, Peter Z a w a d o w ski, John Hallicia, Jacob Sadowski have been other representatives of southern states in the army of George Washington.

On the other side of the American continent U k r a i n i a ns participated in settling of Alaska, many of them unwillingly, as exiles expelled from Ukraine to Siberia and from there transported to the new Russian colony. In 1805 one of these e x i l e s, Demianenko(v), was killed heading an expedition near Yakutat. [10] Four years later another exile from Siberia, a former court clerk, Naplavko(v), plotted to overthrow the rule of the Russian Governor Alexander A. Baranov [11] in Alaska and to establish a republic comprising Kamchatka, Alaska, Aleutian, Kurillen and Hawaiian Islands. The plot was uncovered and Naplavko was sent back to Siberia.

In 1812 the colony Fort Ross was established on the shore of Bodega Bay in California. Its purpose was to supply the settlements in Alaska with grain

8. Daniel Rupp, **Collection of Upwards of 30,000 names of German, Swiss, Dutch, French and other Immigrants in Pennsylvania, 1727-1776,** Philadelphia, 1898.
9. **Pennsylvania in the War of Revolution 1775-1785.** Edited by John Blair Linn, William H. Egle, M. D., Harrisburg, 1880.

10. H. H. Bancroft, **History of Alaska, 1730-1885,** A. L. Bancroft, San Francisco, Cal., 1886.
11. Kiril Khlebnikov, **Zhizneopisanie Alexandra Andreyevicha Baranova** (Biography of A. A. Baranov), St. Petersburg, 1835. Pp. 127-133; H. H. Bancroft, Op. cit., pp. 463-464.

and vegetables. Because of mis-understandings with the Mexican Government the colony was disbanded in 1841 and its land sold to John Sutter, on whose land a few years later gold was discovered. Most of the "Russian" settlers in that colony were from Ukraine. [12]

Returning to the East, scores if not hundreds of Ukrainian names can be found on the rolls of both American armies during the Civil War. The well known historian of the Polish immigration in America, Mieczyslav Haiman [13] took pains of compiling a very imposing list of names, which he considered Polish. In our opinion a good part of them could have belonged to soldiers of Ukrainian as well as Polish extraction (baring a positive proof that they were Polish), and a considerable number of them are purely Ukrainian. For example:

Officers: George Sokalski, Julius Kryvoshinsky, Joseph Krynicki, John Mara, Andrew Ripka, Joseph Pietzuch, Konstantin Nityschi, Michael Walluch. Soldiers: Albert Michnewitsch, Andrew Podolsky, Michael Carahroda, Andrew Gula, Conrad Huba, Anthony Massopust, Ju-

lius Kobierske, Harry Comarnicky, Andrew Czaplensky, Martin Dubrynski, Ambrose Balamut, Bohumil Wehowskey, John Zarewich and others.

It must be pointed out that the above evidence does not give any conclusive proof that the groups and individuals mentioned were of Ukrainian nationality. Nevertheless it shows that there is a well founded basis for supposing that even in those early years of America's growth Ukrainian work and Ukrainian blood participated in the process.

Andreas Ahapius Honcharenko, Ukrainian orthodox priest from Kiev, was the first known Ukrainian immigrant to this country. He arrived in 1865 in the United States, having escaped persecution of the Russian government for his revolutionary connections and activities. [14] In 1868 Honcharenko became editor of the **Alaska Herald**, a bi-monthly in Russian and English, published in San Francisco, Cal., with the help of the American government for enlightenment of the population of the newly acquired territory about American laws. After a few issues Honcharenko began to criticize the condi-

12. A. Mellinkoff, "Russian Colonial Relic" in San Francisco Chronicle, August 24, 1935.

13. Mieczyslaw Haiman, Historja Udzialu Polakow w Amerykanskiej Wojnie Domowej, Chicago, Ill., 1928.

14. Spomynky Ahapiya Honcharenka, Ukrainskoho Kozaka Svyaschennyka (Memoirs of A. Honcharenko, a Ukrainian Cossack-Priest), Kolomea, 1894.

tions in Alaska and the abuses of military authorities perpetrated on the native population. He lost governmental support but carried on his fight and thus contributed to the improvement of administration in the territory. [15] Honcharenko was the first in America to print excerpts from Shevchenko's poems in his newspaper (No. 16). Until death he was active in helping Russian and Ukrainian refugees from Tsarist exile in Siberia. He died on his small farm named "Ukraina" in Hayward, Cal., in 1916. [16]

## Mass Immigration

Ukrainians started to come to the United States in large groups sometime during the seventies of the last century, the first having arrived before or about 1876.

In 1877 the Austrian government issued its first secret circular on emigration, ordering local authorities in the province of Galicia to prevent poor peasants from leaving the country for America.

The Carpathian Mountains of Galicia and of the northern part of Hungary, populated by impoverished [17] Ukrainian peasants provided cheap labor for the immense holdings of Polish and Hungarian landowners. They paid their workers at a rate of eight to twelve American cents a day for fourteen to sixteen hours of work. With the advent of emigration, the landowners became alarmed lest their workers find better conditions elsewhere. [18]

In America at that time industry was recovering from the depression of 1873-1876. In addition, American companies were trying to break the growing union movement of their workers by importing cheap labor from Europe. They made agreements with steamship companies which sent out agents to every section of Europe "to supply employers with European labor in any quantity, anywhere, at any time." [19] Some of these agents reached the Carpathian region of Galicia and Hungary and their successful activities caused the abovementioned scare among the Po-

15. Bancroft, Op. cit., pp. 602, 608, 677.

16. Yaroslav Chyz, "Ahapij Honcharenko," Almanac of the Ukrainian Workingmen's Association, Scranton, 1935, pp. 112-122.

17. In Galicia, in 1893, 4,493 landlords owned 7,637,945 acres of farm land while 1,623,837 peasant families lived on 10,017,274 acres. Out of the 4,493 big landowners, 161 alone possessed 3,782,206 acres. See: Vyacheslav Budzynowsky, Chlopska Posilist (The Land Owned by Peasants), Lwow, 1901, passim.

18. Julian Bachinsky, Ukrainska Immigraciya v Zyedynenych Derzavach Ameriky (Ukrainian Immigration in the United States of America), Lwow, 1914, pp. 3-5.

19. Charles & Mary Beard, The Rise of American Civilization (New York, 1927), II, p. 245.

lish and Hungarian nobles. This resulted in the anti-emigration measures of the Austro - Hungarian government.

The first news about the wages, which were ten to fifteen times higher than those earned at home, together with the tales of political and social freedom, encouraged new groups to emigrate to the New World, in spite of the countermeasures of the Austro - Hungarian government. The Ukrainian immigrants began to arrive in large numbers, first to the coal mines around Shenandoah and Pittsburgh in Pennsylvania, later to all larger American industrial centers. They often suffered derision and even bodily harm from American workers; but the lure of high wages and the ignorance as to what it was all about made them stick to their jobs.

Many paid dearly for their eagerness to reach the Promised Land. They were robbed by fake agents, defrauded by unscrupulous emigration officials, exploited by steamship agencies and their American ossociates. Several hundred were tricked into signing contracts they could not understand and transported to sugar plantations in the Hawaiian Islands (by way of Cape Horn!). After annexation of Hawaii by the United States a special law had to be passed by Congress in 1900 in order to free them from the state of practical slavery.[20] Others became victims of fraudulent land schemes or were shanghaied into mining camps of West Virginia dominated by company police and whip-bosses. The majority, however, became part and parcel of America's working masses, which were soon to ask for higher wages, shorter hours and better working conditions.

Besides poverty and the lure of high wages, political and religious persecution was another cause for Ukrainian emigration. Thousands of young men arrived here from Austria, Hungary and Russia, and in the post-war years also from Roumania and Poland, in order to escape punishment for political offenses or to avoid military conscription. Several thousands of Protestant peasants from the Russian Ukraine — Stundists, a sect somewhat similar to the Mennonites—settled first in Virginia and then in North Dakota, escaping cruel persecution of the Czarist government and of the official Russian Orthodox Church during the decade preceding the first

20. Y. Chyz, "Ukrainski Emigranty na Hawayach" (Ukrainian Immigrants in Hawaii), in **Almanac of the Ukrainian Workingmen's Association for 1936** (Scranton, 1935), pp. 80-92.

Russian revolution of 1905. [21]

## Beginnings of Organizations

Greek Catholic parishes and church brotherhoods were the first forms of organization among the Ukrainian immigrants. In 1884 the first Ukrainian Greek Catholic priest, Reverend John Volansky from Galicia arrived in Shenandoah, Pennsylvania, where in 1885 the first church of that denomination was erected. In 1886 the first Ukrainian newspaper, **America** (at first bi-monthly, then from 1887 to 1889 weekly) made its appearance there. In 1888 the Brotherhood of Saint Nicholas of that city joined the Knights of Labor. [22] Thus the Ukrainian immigrant worker found his place in the ranks of American labor and the Ukrainian immigration began to take shape as a distinct group in the American community.

Ten years after the consecration of the first church in Shenandoah, the Ukrainian immigration had 107 brotherhoods and societies grouped in two fraternal organizations (in the

year 1896). Larger Ukrainian colonies existed in 94 towns and cities; 57 of them were in Pennsylvania, 12 in New York, 9 in Ohio, 6 in New Jersey, 3 in Indiana, 3 in Illinois, one each in Texas, Maryland, Missouri and Colorado; 42 churches — 29 Greek Catholic and 13 Russian Orthodox—were in existence. [23] Three newspapers served these Ukrainian colonies, which grew by leaps and bounds with every ship coming from Europe. These immigrants worked in coal mines (soft coal and anthracite), foundries, textile mills, carpet factories, cigar factories, restaurants, lumber camps, on railroads and farms. [24] All of them, with the exception of the Stundists came with the idea of making some money with which to pay the debts on their farms at home or to buy some land in the native village, to which they intended to return. Most of them, however, stayed in America. [25] In the

21. Andrey Dubovoy & Yaroslav Chyz, "Ukrainski Koloniyi v Nort Dakoti" (Ukrainian Colonies in North Dakota), in **Almanac of the Ukrainian Workingmen's Association**, Scranton, 1936, pp. 134-145. Encyclopedia Britannica, 1911, XXIII, p. 887 a.

22. Count Leliwa (E. N. Matrosov), "Zaokeanskaya Rus" (The Russ Beyond the Ocean), Istorichesky Viestnik (The Herald of History), St. Petersburg, 1897, Vol. 77, 78.

23. Rev. Nestor Dmytriv, ed., Pershij Rusko-Amerikanskyj Kalendar (First Ruthenian-American Almanac), Mount Carmel, Pa., 1897), pp. 160-169.
24. Rev. K. Andruchovich, Z Zhitia Rusyniw v Ameryci (Life of Ruthenians in America), Kolomea, 1904.
25. According to the Annual Reports of the Commissioner General of Immigration for the years 1899 to 1930, 268,421 Ukrainians had arrived in this country. Between 1908 and 1930, 29,305 Ukrainians left the United States. There are no official statistics of immigration and departures by nationalities for previous years.

first place, the agrarian policy of the Austro-Hungarian government, dominated by big landowners, prevented the peasants from buying land. On the other hand, the political freedom and the higher standard of living in America made them reluctant to return to the oppression and misery of their native land.

### Political Divisions

All Ukrainian immigrants resented the oppressive political and economic conditions in their native land, which had forced them to emigrate to America. In the course of their group life in this country most of them formed more or less definite conceptions as to how those c o n d i t i o n s could be changed and improved. The comparison with American institutions and the political freedom of this country contributed largely to the development of those notions and the subsequent political differentiation into sharply defined groups. It is only natural that those groups remained in close contact with the corresponding groups of thought in the "old country." Three main subdivisions, which manifest themselves in political and religious life of Ukrainian immigrants, resulted from these processes.

The first group of thought favors the development of national culture, the promotion of political organization and the strengthening of economic life of the Ukrainian people with an independent Ukrainian state as the ultimate goal. The World War and the subsequent struggle for independence of Ukraine gave a marked impetus to that group, both in Europe and in America. The supporters of those ideals in America insist on using the name "Ukrainian" in place of all other local, provincial or foreign designations. They give considerable support to the movement for independence of Ukraine and to various Ukrainian cultural and political activities in Europe.

The second group had no faith in the idea that anything could be accomplished by endeavors of Ukrainians alone. They turned their eyes towards Russia, the traditional enemy of Austria-Hungary and Poland. This trend was supported by the Russian government, church and civic organizations. Many of this group maintain that the Ukrainian language is but a "Little Russian" dialect of Russian. They pin their hopes on political and cultural unity with Russia and manifest their convictions by calling themselves "Russians" or "Little Russians." After the collapse of the Czarist government they kept in contact with the anti-bolshevik Russian emigration, although some of them try to see in the Soviet Union the heir to the Russia of the Tsars.

The third group is composed mainly of immigrants from Hungary. Their native region was incorporated for 20 years in the Czecho-Slovak Republic as the province of Carpathian Ruthenia and after a short-lived autonomy as Carpatho-Ukraine in 1938-1939 was re-occupied by Hungary in March, 1939. For a long time these Ukrainians were dominated by their Magyarized priests, who strove to preserve their parishioners' blind loyalty to the Hungarian government. They instructed their followers to register as "Hungarians of Greek Catholic faith" and did their best to keep them away from "dangerous" Ukrainian or Russophile tendencies. But since the World War the influence of these Hungarian priests has declined in a large degree and the whole group is becoming more and more interested in the political problems of their countrymen in Europe.

This group is composed of the Ukrainians, who call themselves by the local name of "Roosins" or "Russniaks" (in English Carpatho - Russians or Ruthenians). The immigrants from the westernmost part of Ukrainian territory (Carpathi-

an mountains between the rivers Poprad, San and Uzh), who speak the Lemko dialect of the Ukrainian language, are sometimes referred to and even have some organizations under that name. In general political activities they tend to join the first or the second group.

The above outlined differentiation occurred chiefly among the immigrants from former Austria-Hungary. The less numerous immigrants from formerly Russian Ukraine either stood apart from these processes, as was the case with the Stundists of North Dakota, or joined the first or second group.

The struggle between clericalism and secularism in political and cultural life of Ukrainian immigration group, the appearance and growth of socialist and other progressive movements, communist and fascist propaganda, better understanding of American democracy and the constantly present desire to help Ukraine's independence played important parts in further differentiation of the Ukrainian immigration in the United States.

## Church

The majority of Ukrainian immigrants from Austria-Hungary (except those from the province of Bukovina) were originally of the Greek Catholic religion, which recognizes the

Pope as the head of the Church but retains the Byzantine rite, including the Julian calendar, and the old-Slavonic language in church rituals. In this it is similar to the Orthodox Russian religion, to which the less numerous immigrants from Russian Ukraine belong.

For more than twenty years the Ukrainian parishes in the United States have been under the jurisdiction of the Roman Catholic hierarchy, which treated them with a large measure of intolerance because of a different rite. This circumstance, coupled with the Russophile tendencies of some priests and laymen, induced many parishes to join the Russian Orthodox Church, which more than welcomed the new proselytes. [26] From 1891, when that movement started, to 1917, 169 parishes of former Greek Catholics were organized within the Russian Orthodox Church in America. [27] Many Greek Catholics also joined Orthodox parishes, established by the official Russian Mission for Ukrainian,

Russian and White Russian immigrants from Russia.

The remaining Greek Catholic clergy and parishioners revolted many times against the treatment accorded them by Irish bishops. In 1902, after a conference of the Greek Catholic clergy in Harrisburg, Pennsylvania, a movement "Away from Rome" began to take definite shape. This and other reasons, among them being the rapid increase in Ukrainian immigration, brought about the establishment of a Greek Catholic Diocese in the United States with a separate Bishop of Ukrainian nationality, in 1907. Later on the tendency of the clergy from former Hungary to be independent of "Ukrainian influences" and the desire of Czecho-Slovakia to have the immigrants from their newly acquired province of Carpathian Ruthenia under separate jurisdiction resulted in the creation of a separate "Ruthenian" Diocese with a bishop for Greek Catholic immigrants from former Hungary. The seat of the Ukrainian-Catholic bishop is in Philadelphia, of the "Ruthenian"-Catholic in Pittsburgh, Pa.

The establishment of these separate dioceses for Ukrainian catholics in the United States did not stop the movement "Away from Rome." A

---

26. Yuvyleyniy Almanach Ukrainskoi Hreko-Katolyckoi Cerkwy w Zluchenych Derzhavach 1884 - 1934 (Jubilee Book of the Ukrainian Greek Catholic Church in the United States, 1884-1934), Philadelphia, 1934, p. 105.

27. Russko - Amerykansky Pravoslawny Kalendar na 1936 God (Russian American Orthodox Almanac for the year 1936). Published by the Russian Orthodox Mutual Aid Society, Wilkes-Barre, Pa., 1935, p. 112.

Ukrainian Orthodox church organization was started which in 1921 developed into the Ukrainian Autocephalous Orthodox Diocese with its bishop connected with the supreme hierarchy of that Church in Kiev. The Ukrainian language was introduced in church services in place of the old-Slavonic together with the participation of laymen in the administration of affairs of the Diocese.

Several years later (during 1928-1929) another Ukrainian Orthodox Church and Diocese was organized by a group of priests who, for various reasons, left the Greek Catholic Church without joining the Ukrainian Autocephalous Orthodox Diocese. They organized themselves into the Ukrainian Orthodox D i o c e s e connected with the Orthodox Patriarch in Istambul, Turkey. The seat of the bishop is in New York City.

Finally a similar split occurred in the Ruthenian Diocese of Pittsburgh, from which several parishes and their priests separated into a Greek Catholic Diocese of Eastern Rite with a bishop ordained in 1939 by the Patriarch in Istambul and with its seat in Bridgeport, Conn.

In the ten Russian Orthodox Dioceses in the United States 80 per cent of parishes are composed exclusively or in a great majority of former Greek Catholics or of immigrants from former Russian Ukraine and Austrian Bukóvina.

In all these religious groupings and regroupings the dogmatic part of the church teachings was of no primary importance. The national, political and often personal and materialistic reasons frequently determined the changes of church allegiance of some priests and lay leaders.

The Protestant missions have made little headway among the Ukrainians. There are more than score of their congregations with Ukrainian ministers and pastors, twelve of them (Baptists, Adventists and Mennonites) among the former "Shtoondisty" in North Dakota. Few Presbyterian and Methodist groups, together with several Baptist churches, are scattered throughout the East.

There is considerable difficulty in making an estimate of the numerical strength of each church group. The following discussion is based on statistical data and estimates for the years 1934-1935, since for those years most of the material is available.

Official statistics of the above church organizations (except the Greek-Catholic Church of Eastern Rite) were at that time as follows:

The Ukrainian Catholic Diocese claimed 89 priests, 127 churches and 264,685 members. [28] The Ruthenian (Pittsburgh) Diocese claimed 120 priests, 166 churches and 280,333 members. [29] The Russian Orthodox Church reported 221 churches with 194 priests in communities with Ukrainian colonies. The membership for all Russian Orthodox Churches and chapels in the United States, Alaska and Canada was given as 325,000. [30] The Ukrainian Autocephalous Orthodox Church had 27 priests, 28 churches, and 15,925 members (counting five persons to a family). [31] The Ukrainian Orthodox Diocese was credited with 30 priests, 30 churches (three of them in Canada), and 10,000 members. [32]

Some of the official statistics are not accurate. The Catholic churches consider all persons baptized in the Catholic faith as their members unless they have renounced such membership by formal act. However, very few of the Orthodox Ukrainians in America have gone through that formality and probably are carried on the rolls of both Greek Catholic Dioceses, although by thousands they have joined various Orthodox and other church organizations. On the other hand, the Russian Orthodox Church reported in 1926, 199 active churches with 95,134 members. [33] The later number of 325,000 members would mean an increase of 230,000 new members in nine years, which sounds improbable. The statement of the same source that the Ukrainian Orthodox Church had in 1935 only 10,000 members in thirty churches was undoubtedly an underestimate.

On the basis of other more reliable sources, [34] the following very conservative estimate of the membership of Ukrainians in the above church organizations in 1935 was obtained:

28. Official Catholic Directory for 1935, P. J. Kennedy and Son, New York, pp. 639-642.

29. Ibid., pp. 643-647. The Greek Catholic Pittsburgh Diocese listed at that time 179 churches with 133 priests and 301,197 members. 20,866 members and 13 priests have been deducted for the 13 Hungarian and Croatian Greek Catholic churches belonging to the Diocese.

30. Russian American Orthodox Almanac for 1936, pp. 143 and 159.

31. Letter to the author by the Rt. Rev. Johannes Theodorovich, Bishop of the Ukrainian Autocephalous Orthodox Church.

32. Russian American Orthodox Almanac for 1936, p. 159.

33. Census of Religious Bodies, 1926 (Department of Commerce, Bureau of the Census, 1929), Vol. II, pp. 507-515.

34. The 50-Year Jubilee Almanac of the Ukrainian Greek Catholic Church in the United States (Philadelphia, 1935); Census of Religious Bodies, 1926; Letter of Rt. Rev. Johannes Theodorovich; The lists of Parishes in the Official Catholic Directory; Reports of various Ukrainian Fraternal Organizations.

|                                                      | members   |
|------------------------------------------------------|-----------|
| The Ukrainian Greek Catholic Church                  | 95,000    |
| The Ruthenian Greek Catholic Diocese                 | 135,500   |
| The Ukrainians in the Russian Orthodox Dioceses      | 110,000   |
| The Ukrainian Orthodox Autocephalous Diocese         | 16,000    |
| The Ukrainian Orthodox Church                        | 16,500    |
| The Independent Churches of Greek Rite               | 1,500     |
| The Presbyterians, Baptists, Adventists, etc.        | 15,000    |
| Total                                                | 389,500   |

The Ukrainian Greek-Catholic Diocese uses as its printed organ the monthly **Misionar,** Philadelphia, Pa., founded in 1914. The Ukrainian Autocephalous Orthodox Church publishes a bi-monthly **Dnipro,** Philadelphia, Pa. (founded in 1922). **Ukrainsky Vistnyk** (Ukrainian Herald, 1929) of Carteret, N. J., is the press organ of the Ukrainian Orthodox diocese, and the weekly **Vistnik-Messenger,** Pittsburgh, Penna. (founded in 1936) of the Greek-Catholics of Eastern Rite.

### Fraternal Organizations

Although the first attempt to organize a fraternal association among the Ukrainian immigrants (The Greek Catholic Union, 1887) was unsuccessful, the advantages of such organization were too evident and five years later another attempt was made. The Ukrainian immigrants discovered that fraternal societies were the best-suited form of permanent organization. The insurance features of such societies (death and sick benefits) induce the members to stay in the organization. The printed organ provides the means of expression, communication of news, propaganda and literary entertainment. The union of lodges (assemblies and branches) from various localities and states gives the feeling of united strength and creates the desire of activity in other than the fraternal field.

It was, therefore, natural that various political and religious groups either founded their own fraternal associations or tried to assume control of the existing ones. Thus every new grouping among Ukrainian immigrants resulted almost invariably in the split of an old or in the formation of a new fraternal society. Outside of Orthodox or Catholic, progressive or conservative, secular or clerical differences, the main division of these organizations goes along the previously described lines: there are definitely Ukrainian organizations, fraternal associations of immigrants from

Carpathian Ukraine, who most often call themselves Carpatho-Russians or Ruthenians, and societies of Russophile Ukrainians who call themselves Russians.

The GREEK CATHOLIC UNION OF RUSSIAN BROTHERHOODS (Sojedinenie Greko-Kaftoliceskych Russkich Bratstv), founded in 1892, has become the largest benevolent organization of the Carpatho-Russian-Ruthenian group, and the UKRAINIAN NATIONAL ASSOCIATION (Ukrayinsky Narodny Soyuz), Jersey City, N. J., founded in 1894, of the Ukrainian group. The Russophile and Orthodox propaganda among Ukrainian immigrants in America resulted in the founding of two separate Russophile organizations in 1895 and 1900 respectively. The refusal of the members of the Greek Catholic Union to be dominated exclusively by the priests brought about a secession of some of the latter and the founding of the UNITED SOCIETIES OF GREEK CATHOLIC RELIGION (Sobranie Greko Katoliceskich Cerkownych Bratstv) in 1903. Conflict between clerical and progressive forces in the Ukrainian National Association in 1910 caused the secession of the progressive and socialist members and gave origin to the UKRAINIAN WORKINGMEN'S ASSOCIA-

TION (Ukrainsky Robitnychy Soyuz), which holds to its democratic and progressive policies ever since. In 1913 the Catholic PROVIDENCE ASSOCIATION OF UKRAINIAN CATHOLICS IN AMERICA (Provydinnia, Stovaryshennia Ukrainciv Katolykiv v Ameryci) was organized, and in 1915 the UKRAINIAN NATIONAL AID ASSOCIATION (Ukrainska Narodna Pomich) came into being.

Minor splits brought about the founding of a half dozen smaller organizations, some of them regional in character. After unsuccessful attempts to dominate some of the existing organizations the communists founded the Ukrainian and the Carpatho-Russian sections of the INTERNATIONAL WORKERS' ORDER in 1932.

Two organizations, which ceased to exist, deserve mentioning. ST. OLGA SISTERHOOD (Sestryctwo Swiatoi Olhy), which existed in New York and vicinity from 1897 to 1907, [35] was the first Ukrainian women's organization in America; and the FRATERNAL ORGANIZATION HAJDAMAKY (1910-1918) played for some time quite an important

---

35. **Yuvilejnyj Almanach Ukrainskoi Zhinochoi Hromady w New Yorku** (Jubilee Almanac of the Ukrainian Ladies Society of New York), New York, 1931, pp. 77-78.

role in the development of Ukrainian progressive thought in this country.

## Fraternal Membership

Each fraternal organization has its press organ, which usually represents a distinct political trend. The respective fraternal strength can be summed up for each group in round numbers [36] as follows:

The larger Ukrainian and Ruthenian (C a r p a t ho-Russian) fraternal associations had in 1939 about 146,000 members and over 21 million dollars assets. They were:

Ukrainian National Association, Jersey City, N. J., press organs **Svoboda**, daily, and **Ukrainian Weekly** (in English); Ukrainian Workingmen's Association, Scranton, Pa., **Narodna Wola**, tri-weekly; Providence Association, Philadelphia, Pa., **America**, tri-weekly; Ukrainian National Aid Association, Pittsburgh, Pa., **Narodne Slowo**, weekly. Combined membership — 56,000; combined assets — about 10 million dollars.

Greek Catholic Union, Homestead, Pa., press organ **Amerikansko-Russky Viestnik**, weekly; United Societies of the Greek Catholic Religion, McKeesport, Pa., **Prosvita**, weekly; United Russian Orthodox Brotherhood, founded in 1915, Pittsburgh, Pa., **Russky Vistnik**, weekly; Russian Orthodox Fraternity "Lubov," Mayfield, Pa., **Lubov**, monthly. — Combined membership about 90,000; combined assets — over 11 million dollars.

The two Russophile organizations were:

Russian Brotherhood Organization, Philadelphia, Pa., press organ **Pravda**, bi-weekly; Russian Orthodox Catholic Mutual Aid, Wilkes-Barre, Pa., **Svit**, weekly. Combined membership — over 25,000; combined assets over 3 million dollars.

With the several smaller organizations as well as the Ukrainian [37] and Carpatho-Russian sections of the International Workers' Order the fraternal membership of Ukrainians in this country can be put at — 200,000. The assets of their fraternal organizations in 1939 amounted well over 25 million dollars.

36. For exact data and annual changes in membership and assets of most of the above mentioned associations see: A. S. Hamilton, **Statistics Fraternal Societies**, published annually by the Fraternal Monitor, 537 Powers Building, Rochester, N. Y.; **The Fraternal Compend Digest**, published jointly by Taylor, Bird & Co., 18 Inter-Ocean Bldg., Cedar Rapids, Iowa, and the National Underwriter Company, 420 East Fourth St., Cincinnati, Ohio.

37. The Ukrainian Section of the I. W. O. uses the daily **Ukrainski Schodenni Wisty**, New York, N. Y., as their organ.

## Other Organizations

Many local and national societies and associations promote social and cultural life of the Ukrainian immigrants and give support to various political causes. From several such national organizations the more important are:

DEFENSE OF UKRAINE (Oborona Ukrainy), with its headquarters in Scranton, Pa., and with branches in all larger cities with Ukrainian colonies. It supports progressive and democratic political groups in Ukraine and among Ukrainian emigres in Europe. It publishes a monthly **Orhanizaciyni Wisty Oborony Ukrainy** (Organizational Herald of Defense of Ukraine), a party bulletin.

UNITED UKRAINIAN ORGANIZATIONS (Obyednannia Ukrainskich Orhanizaciy) comprises the representatives of the fraternal Ukrainian National Association, The Ukrainian Legion, Organization For Rebirth of Ukraine, Ukrainian National Women's League, Ukrainian Youth League and few others. Being the "political arm" of the Ukrainian National Association, it uses the daily **Svoboda** and the **Ukrainian Weekly** as its mouthpiece, and is dominated by officers of the Association. UNITED ORGANIZATIONS serve chiefly as intermediary in sending contribu-

tions to various institutions and political groups in Europe. In its policies they follow much the ideology of the

ORGANIZATION FOR REBIRTH OF UKRAINE (Orhanizaciya Derzhavnoho Vidrodzhennia Ukrainy), which in turn supports the policies of the Organization of Ukrainian Nationalists with headquarters in Vienna and with a prominently totalitarian platform. The ORGANIZATION FOR REBIRTH OF UKRAINE has its headquarters in New York. It publishes a Ukrainian weekly, **Ukraina** (formerly **Nationalist**), and an English monthly, **The Trident**.

UNION OF UKRAINIAN WORKERS' SOCIETIES (Soyuz Ukrainskich Robitnichych Orhanizaciy) tries to spread Stalinism among the Ukrainian sympathizers of the Soviet Union; it uses the Communist daily **Ukrainski Schodenni Wisty** (Ukrainian Daily News) for its press organ.

UNITED HETMAN ORGANIZATIONS (Soyuz Hetmanciv Derzhavnykiv), with headquarters in Chicago, Ill., and with the weekly **Nash Stiah** (Our Way), promote monarchist ideas among the Ukrainian immigrants.

BLACK SEA COSSACKS ASS'N (Chornomorska Sitch), with headquarters in New York, cultivates Ukrainian patriotic spirit among the members of its branches. It p u b l i s h e s monthly **Sichovy Klich** (The Sitch Call) quite irregularly.

UKRAINIAN LEGION (Striletska Hromada), New York, N. Y., unites several scores of veterans of Ukrainian wars now in this country.

THE UKRAINIAN NATIONAL WOMEN'S LEAGUE (Soyuz Ukrainok Ameriky), with branches in larger Ukrainian settlements and with its headquarters in New York, promotes educational and social activities among Ukrainian women. The executive committee as well as several branches must be credited with numerous expositions of Ukraine's folk art in American cities, held usually under the auspices of other American women's organizations, such as the Y. W. C. A., the National Women's League, etc.

DEFENSE OF LEMKO LAND ASSOCIATION (Orhanizaciya Oborony Lemkivschiny), New York, publishes a monthly **Lemkivsky Dzvin** (Lemko Bell) and conducts activities aimed at cultural support of their countrymen in Europe and their union with free Ukraine.

THE LEMKO ASSOCIATION of New York City spreads Russophile and pro-Soviet ideas among the immigrants from Lemko-land; its pro-Communist bi-weekly **Lemko** appears in the local dialect of that region in New York City.

THE UKRAINIAN YOUTH LEAGUE OF NORTH AMERICA promotes knowledge of Ukraine among the second and third generations of Ukrainians in this country. It has educational and sport departments and its executive committee published in English a progressive monthly, **The Ukrainian Trend.** After change of officials in 1939 the monthly and the progressiveness disappeared.

THE UKRAINIAN CATHOLIC YOUTH LEAGUE has the same purpose, but it limits its membership to Catholics only. It voices its aims through the **Ukrainian Youth,** an English monthly. — THE LEAGUE OF UKRAINIAN CLUBS was an Orthodox Organization, which used the "English Page" of the **Ukrainian Herald,** a monthly organ of the Ukrainian Orthodox Diocese; in 1939 it ceased to exist. Both of these organizations were under the influence of the clergy.

Several national organizations of Ukrainians have ceased existing. Most of them came to life and were most active during the World War and in the immediate post-war period. Their activities concerned themselves mainly with the problems of Ukraine in Europe.

The UKRAINIAN FEDER-ATION OF THE UNITED STATES was formed in 1916. It obtained a proclamation from President Wilson, whereby April 21, 1917, was officially declared "Ukrainian Relief Day." The substantial collections of that day were used through the American Red Cross to relieve the starvation of war-ridden Ukraine. The representatives of the Ukrainian Federation participated along with the representatives of the Czechs, Slovaks, Poles, Carpatho-Russians, Lithuanians and others, then oppressed nationalities, in an impressive ceremony on October 26, 1918, in Philadelphia, at which, under the leadership of Professor Thomas Garrigue Masaryk, the right of self-determination of these nationalities was proclaimed.

A parallel organization, the UKRAINIAN ALLIANCE IN AMERICA, also conducted propaganda for Ukrainian independence at that time. It published several pamphlets and sent its representative to Paris at the time of the Peace Conference. The rivalry between the Federation and Alliance was very bitter.

THE CARPATHO-RUSSIAN NATIONAL COUNCIL in the United States conducted among the immigrants from Carpatho-Ukraine a plebiscite in order to determine where their country should belong after the collapse of Austria-Hungary. Sixty-eight per cent of all votes were cast for Czechoslovakia, twenty-eight for Ukraine, one per cent for Russia and Hungary, and two per cent for full independence. On the basis of these results the Council passed on July 23 and November 12, 1918, a resolution demanding that their country be separated from Hungary and united with Czechoslovakia. [38] This induced their compatriots in Europe to agree to the creation of Carpathian Ruthenia as an autonomous province of the Czechoslovak Republic.

Outside of the above-mentioned national organizations and their local branches, the American Ukrainians have formed many local societies. In more than 100 Ukrainian communities in the United States "national homes" were built or bought with a hall for mass meetings, amateur shows, concerts and lectures, and with rooms for evening schools, clubs and other social purposes. In many communities "the hall under the church" is put to the

---

38. E. Benes, The Carpatho-Russian Problem, Prague, 1934; Podkarpatska Rus, Edited by J. Chmelar, Stan. Klima, J. Necas New York, 1924, pp. 7-15; T. G. Masaryk, The Makings of a State, London, 1927, pp. 238-241.

same use. Local reading clubs (often called "Prosvita" — Enlightenment), gymnastic societies called "Sitch" (from the name of an ancient Cossack fortress) or "Sokol" (Falcon), welfare societies, athletic clubs and other associations, together with fraternal lodges and assemblies, hold their meetings in such "national homes" or "Ukrainian community centers." Almost every Ukrainian colony has one or more "citizens' clubs" through which American citizens of Ukrainian birth and descent participate in local politics.

There have been several more or less successful attempts to bring all Ukrainian citizens' clubs of a state or of a county into a sort of union or league. Such state-wide organizations exist in New York and New Jersey. County or inter-county leagues are active in Pennsylvania (Lackawanna, Luzerne, A l l e g h e n y, Schuylkill and Northumberland counties), in Ohio, Michigan and Illinois. They often succeed in placing their members in municipal, county and state offices. A Ukrainian attorney was deputy attorney-general in Pennsylvania, the same position is held by another Ukrainian lawyer in the state of Michigan. Schuylkill County has several county and local officers of Ukrainian de-

scent. Olyphant, Pa., has its second Lemko Burgess, and the Eight Assembly District in New York is for the third term represented in Albany by an American Ukrainian.

S e p a r a t e Ukrainian party units existed before 1919 in the Socialist Party of America and afterwards, after the bolshevik upheaval, [39] in the American Communist Party.

For instant action, mostly on behalf of Ukrainians abroad, special committies are often formed. They arrange for local or regional protest meetings, street demonstrations and other manifestations of the collective feeling and will. In one such action, namely, for liberation of Miroslav Sichinsky from the Austrian jail, over 30,000 signatures were collected on a petition demanding his release. [40] Manifestations for Ukrainian independence in 1918-1920 brought tens of thousands of Ukrainians on the streets of New York, Philadelphia, Detroit, Chicago and other cities. The same happened during the infamous "pacification" of Western Ukraine [41] by the Polish

39. M. Nastasivsky, U k r a i n s k a Imihraciya v Spoluchenych Derzhavach (Ukrainian Immigration in the United States), published by the Union of Ukrainian Workers' Societies, New York, 1934, pp. 148-161.

40. Narodna Wola, Scranton, Pa., No. 29, 1911.

41. See: Emil Revyuk, Polish At-

government in 1930. According to incomplete tabulation 160 mass meetings were held by Ukrainians at that time in 94 cities with an estimated attendance of 104,000 persons. [42]

Through the efforts of Ukrainian societies and fraternal organizations the Ukrainian Pavilion was erected in 1933 at the Chicago World's Fair, which was one of the most picturesque attractions of the Fair. [43]

Government-caused starvation and death to some four million peasants in Soviet Ukraine evoked vigorous protests and manifestations, often with bloody encounters with communist counter-demonstrations, as was the case in Boston, Chicago, New York, Detroit, Bridgeport and other cities during Winter and Spring of 1933-1934. [44]

The events in Carpatho-Ukraine in 1938-1939 caused similar action on the part of American Ukrainians as did the "pacification" and other previous events in the political life of Ukrainians in Europe.

Outside of these sporadic actions, the Ukrainian immigration constantly gave aid to the cultural, political and humanitarian institutions in their "old country," especially after the World War. Over fifty thousand dollars was sent in 1920-1922 to the Ukrainian Citizens' Committee in Lwiw for Ukrainian refugees, invalids, war widows and orphans, political prisoners and destitute farmers in villages destroyed by war. Clothes and other supplies, worth more than 30,000 dollars, were delivered to the same Committee by the American Red Cross, which was bought for money collected by the Ukrainian Federation in America.

A dormitory for girl pupils of vocational schools in Lwiw [45] and two buildings for Ukrainian workers' societies, [46] as well as the Home for Ukrainian War Invalids in the same city have been bought from funds collected in the United States and Canada. Over 100,000 dollars

rocities in Ukraine, United Ukrainian Organizations, New York, 1931; Samuel Wallace and Yaroslav Chyz, Western Ukraine under Polish Yoke, published by Ukrainian Review, New York, 1931.

42. Ukrainian Review, New York, N. Y., May, 1931.

43. V. Levitsky, "Uchast Ukrainciv u Shikagovskiy Vystavci" (Ukrainian Participation in the Chicago Fair), Jubilee Almanac of the Ukrainian Workingmen's Association for 1935, Scranton, 1934, pp. 129-136.

44. The Boston Globe, Nov. 13, 1933; Chicago Daily Tribune, Dec. 18, 1933; New York Herald-Tribune, November 19, 1933; Detroit Free Press, Nov. 5, 1933; Bridgeport Post, Nov. 27, 1933.

45. Almanac of The Ukrainian Ladies Society in New York, New York, 1931.

46. Almanac of the Ukrainian Workingmen's Ass'n for 1936, Scranton, 1935, pp. 130-131.

have been collected between 1923-1939 for medical help to and maintenance of those invalids among American Ukrainians. [47] The popular publishing cooperative "Samoosvita" (Self-Enlightenment) was founded on and aided with funds from progressive groups of Ukrainians in America. It published over 110 booklets on various academic subjects — altogether more than 500,000 copies — inside of nine years. Private schools [48] and other educational societies and institutions, among them for some time the Ukrainian Academy of Science in Kiev, received help from Ukrainian immigrants.

The most important aid given by Ukrainian immigrants to the country of their birth was probably their assistance in building village cultural centers, so-called "chytalni" (reading clubs). It can be said without exaggeration that hundreds of those centers would not have been built, not even started,

without funds and prompting from American countrymen. Such village "national homes" became centers of cultural and economic activity and played a very important part in lifting the peasants in Western Ukraine to a higher cultural level and in strengthening their resistance to Polish oppression. At the same time, correspondence with villagers concerning the "national home" and its activities, exchange of news and plans carried many an American idea into Ukrainian villages abroad. The more so that those ideas came often together with help after floods or during famines. Although not too abundant, it was in most cases the only outside aid in dire distress and misery.

It must be admitted that some of the support to various Ukrainian causes was given more generously than wisely. Hundreds of thousands of dollars have been collected in 1918-1919 (about — $150,000.00), [49] 1921-1923 (about $140,000.00) [50] and up to 1939 (between 80 and 90 thousand dollars) for various schemes purporting "liberation of Ukraine," which were of little if any value, if not out-

47. Lev Yasinchuk in Propamiatna Knyha Ukrainskoho Narodnoho Soyuza (Jubilee Book of the U.N.A), Dr. Luke Myshuha, editor., Jersey City, N. J., 1936, pp. 373-374; Kalendar "Ukrainsky Invalid" na Rik 1936 (Almanac "Ukrainian Invalid" for 1936), published by Ukrainian Invalid Help Ass'n, Lwiw, 1935, pp. 19-20, and same Almanac for 1937, p. 28; Quarterly "Ukrainsky Invalid," Lwiw, May 1939, p. 8.

48. Lev Yasinchuk, Op. cit., pp. 372-373, and Za Okeanom (Beyond the Ocean), Lwiw, 1930.

49. Lev Yasinchuk, Jubilee Book of the U. N. A., p. 370.

50. Rev. P. Poniatishin on "Ukrainian Church and the U. N. Ass'n," Jubilee Book of the U. N. Association, p. 298.

rightly detrimental to the Ukrainian cause. Probably not less than $100,000 was collected and spent for various communist purposes.

All this activity on behalf of Ukraine and almost all of the above collections took place among Ukrainian immigrants outside of the Carpatho-Russian and Russophile groups. There was an attempt on the part of the Russophiles to arrange for a "Russian Day" similar to the "Ukrainian Day" of 1917, but even that attempt failed.

### Cultural Life

Very popular manifestations of the cultural life of Ukrainian immigrants are the amateur shows. The plays and operettas like "Natalka Poltavka," "Zaporozhetz za Dunayem" (translated into English),[51] "Kateryna" and others usually represent the Ukrainian life as it was in the old country. Some amateur troupes have reached a very high artistic level especially when directed by professional actors, many of whom came to America after the World War.

Another form of the artistic expression of Ukrainian immigrants and their children are

concerts, usually in commemoration of Ukrainian poets Taras Shevchenko[52] (born March 8, 1814, died March 9, 1861) and Ivan Franko (born August 15, 1856, died May 28, 1916)[53] or important events of recent Ukrainian history, such as the proclamation of Ukrainian independence on January 22nd, 1918, or of independence of Western Ukraine on November 1, 1918. Vocal solos, choral singing, a lecture, sometimes violin or piano solos, or orchestras constitute the usual programs; works of Ukrainian composers and folk songs are rendered. Occasionally such concerts serve as means to show how much the young generation knows about Ukraine; children and youngsters recite Ukrainian poems, present short shows, sing or display their talents as dancers or musicians.

Choral singing has been cultivated among Ukrainian immigrants from the very beginning of their organized life in this country. It became nationally known after two successful tours of the Ukrainian National Chorus, led by Professor Al-

51. Simen Artemovsky, **Cossacks Beyond the Danube**, translated from Ukrainian by W. J. Stepankowsky, New York, 1937.

52. D. Doroshenko, **Taras Shevchenko**, preface by Clarence A. Manning, published by United Ukrainian Organizations, New York, 1936.

53. Percival Cundy, **A Voice From Ukrainia**, Biographical Sketch and Translations From the Works of IVAN FRANKO, R. E. Buffy & Company, Roland, Manitoba, 1932.

exander Koshetz, in 1922-1923. The reception given them by American critics can be judged by the following few excerpts. **The New York Sun:** "Exactness of attack that makes gorgeous hearing . . ."; **Boston Evening Transcript:** "There is nothing remotely approaching it in any choral singing to which the western world is accustomed..."; **The Pittsburgh Post:** "Koshetz sculpts in rhythms . . ."; **Rochester Times Union:** "Marvelous precision of attack that defies description . . ."; **Chicago Evening American:** "Choir of peerless ensemble . . ."; **Washington Herald:** "They plucked at our heart strings . . ." [54]

Professor A. Koshetz and some of his pupils remained in this country. Their work together with the standard set by his original chorus brought Ukrainian choral singing in America to a very high level. Community and church choirs in Metropolitan New York, Scranton, Olyphant, Detroit, Chicago, Pittsburgh, Rochester and other cities have made names for themselves among Americans in general, often far beyond their localities and even states.

Folk dances are also cultivated by Ukrainian immigrants.

54. Chants d' Ukraine, Voix de la Presse, published by Ukrainian Music Society, Paris, 1929, pp. 60-77.

Mainly because of the initiative of the Ukrainian master of that art, Vassile Avramenko, during the last fifteen years several scores of dancing schools and dancing clubs have been organized. Probably close to 10,000 children of Ukrainian immigrants were graduated from such schools and courses conducted by Avramenko and his helpers and acquired knowledge of "Arkan," Kozachok," "Kateryna," "Metelytzia," "Zaporozhsky Hertz" and other dances of Ukraine.

Two high schools and several day schools are maintained by both Greek Catholic dioceses. Between three and four hundred evening classes are supported by Ukrainian communities, where the Ukrainian language and history is taught to the children and grandchildren of Ukrainian immigrants. Probably not less than three-fourths of those schools are maintained by church communities

### Press

During the fifty-two years from 1886 to 1938 Ukrainians published 135 newspapers. Six of them have been dailies, four bi- and tri-weeklies, 36 weeklies, 24 semi - monthlies, 44 monthlies and 22 irregulars or unknown. Several of them merged, more ceased to appear. At the present time the Ukrainian immigration is served by 32 newspapers, two of them dailies, two tri-weeklies, two bi-weeklies, ten weeklies, five semi-monthlies, eight monthlies and three irregular publications. Besides newspapers mentioned previously weeklies **Ukrainska Zoria** (Ukrainian Star) and **Nova Pora** (The New Time) are published in Detroit, Mich., and bi-monthlies **Rodina** (The Family) in Cleveland, Ohio, **Novyj Straz** (The New Sentinel) in Binghamton, N. Y., and **Vostok** in Perth Amboy, N. J.

Twenty-one newspapers belong to the Ukrainian group; four of them are publishèd in English. The Carpatho-Russian group has seven newspapers printed in Ukrainian mountain dialects with an admixture of old-Slavonic and Russian words. Four newspapers, three of them in Russian and in Ukrainian jargon, and one in English, are published by the Russophiles. [55]

From 1896, when the first Ukrainian booklet and almanac in America were published, hundreds of books and pamphlets in both Ukrainian and English, have been issued by

55. Yaroslav Chyz, "Piv Stolittia Ukrayinskoyi Presy v Ameryci" (Half Century of Ukrainian Press in America), Almanac of the Ukrainian Workingmen's Association for 1939. Scranton, 1938, pp. 117-128; Wasyl Halich, Ph. D., Ukrainians in the United States, The University of Chicago Press, Chicago, Ill., 1937, pp. 111-124; Julian Bachinsky, Op. cit., pp. 443-464.

various Ukrainian societies, committees, organizations and individuals. Part of those publications were devoted to enlightenment of i m m i g r a n t s themselves on various subjects, mostly political. Scores of booklets and pamphlets were printed to acquaint the American public with the problems of Ukraine. The largest group of publications consists of annual almanacs issued by fraternal organizations and containing usually a calendarium, various timely informations, few short stories and poems and educational articles.

## Contributions to American Life

The Ukrainian immigration contributed to the material and cultural development of America by honest work performed daily by hundreds of thousands of men and women of Ukrainian birth and descent, by artistic and scientific contributions of their more gifted individuals and by introducing into the American pattern many cultural values of their native land.

The work in mines, foundries, mills, factories, and in all other occupations, was performed according to American standards and methods. It was not better and not worse than the performance of workers of other nationalities, native Americans included. In some cases, especially in mining and in foundries, the Ukrainian worker and his Slavonic brethren have shown greater endurance than others. This endurance was also the reason that after four attempts to organize a labor union among the coal miners in Pennsylvania failed, the Slavonic peasants who came to the coal pits by their discipline and persistance helped to win the first big strikes (1900 and 1902) in the hard coal region and to establish permanently the organization of United Mine Workers of America. [56]

The famous sculptor Alexander Archipenko and conductor and composer Alexander Koshetz head the list of individuals who have contributed greatly to the Ukrainian as well as American cultures. Mr. Archipenko's masterpieces [57] adorn several American museums of modern art. Many of them have been created in his studios in California and on Long Island. The exposition of his works in the Ukrainian Pavilion at the Chicago World's Fair was considered by critics as one of the main artistic attractions of the fair. The busts of Ukrainian poets T. Shevchenko and I. Franko and of the Kiev prince of 10th century, Vladimir the Great, adorn now the Ukrainian section of the Cultural Garden in Cleveland, Ohio.

The work of Alexander Koshetz was mentioned already in this article. He is still active as conductor of several combined Ukrainian choirs in New York and vicinity, and has published many arrangements of Ukrainian songs for American choirs. Thanks to very good translations into English they are becoming more and more popular with the singers and conductors of American choirs in the United States, Canada and England. [58] Prof. Koshetz arranged also the musical score for the moving picture "Marussia" produced by Ukrainians in this country.

Besides arrangements and compositions of A. Koshetz, works of Michael Hayvoronsky, Roman Prydatkevytch, and Pavlo Pecheniha-Ouglitzky are often heard from Ukrainian and non-Ukrainian stages in America. All three of them live in or around New York and have made names for themselves not only among their Ukrainian countrymen. [59]

56. Samuel Yellen, American Labor Struggles, Harcourt, Brace & Co., New York, 1936; Frank Julian Warne, The Slav Invasion of the Mine Workers, Lippincott, Philadelphia, 1904, p. 93.

57. Prof. Dr. Hans Hildebrandt, Alexander Archipenko, U k r a i n ske Slovo Publ. Ltd., Berlin-Schoenberg, 1923.

58. Songs of the Ukraine, arranged for chorus by Alexander Koshetz, Witmark Educational Publication, New York, N. Y.

59. Michael Hayvoronsky, "Nasha

Among the performers the movie star Anna Sten is daughter of a Swedish mother and Ukrainian father. Concert and opera singers Maria Hrebinetzka, Maria Sokil, Olga Lepka, Mychaylo Holinsky, Peter Ordynsky, pianist-composer and symphony orchestra conductor Anthony Rudnicky, are often heard at concerts or on the radio. Alexander Kulpak is a member of the Chicago Opera Company. New York opera goers still remember performances of Adam Didur, a Ukrainian by birth, and the Philadelphians those of Ivan Steshenko.

Cartoons by John Rosol (Rosolovich) of Philadelphia are enjoyed by millions of readers of American magazines, especially of the Saturday Evening Post. Vladimir Tytla assisted Walter Disney in his masterpiece, "Snow White and Seven Dwarfs." Maria Nahirna won herself a place among American sketchers. Stern Byzantine ikons by late Rev. Gleb Verchovsky can be admired in Ukrainian Catholic churches in Chicago, Scranton and other cities.

In sports Dr. George Kojac of New York established the Olympic record in back stroke swimming in Amsterdam in

1928 and keeps it up 'till now. Football and wrestling star Bronko Nagurski has become an all-time legend of the American gridiron, famous "Gazook-Gazella" (Michael Guzelak) is still remembered among the baseball fans. Peter Fick and John Trepak rank among the best American swimmers and weight lifters respectively.

Dr. Nicholas Konstantinovich Sudzylovsky-Russel, a native of Kiev, was first president of the Hawaiian senate after the incorporation of Hawaii into the United States in 1898.

Sabin A. Sochocky's invention of radium paint and the subsequent manufacture of luminous watch hands brought about his untimely death from radium poisoning. [60] Young Mirko Paneyko's equipment for acoustic electrical sound reproduction, installed in Harvard and Columbia Universities and several other auditoriums in this country, enables the audience to hear reproduced music without distortion of the tone or the presence of extraneous sounds.[61] Volodimir Tymoshenko's works on economic problems of Ukraine and Russia secured for him a professorship first at the University of Michigan and lat-

---

Muzyka v Ameryci" (Our Music in America), Jubilee Book of the U. N. Ass'n, pp. 431-439.

60. New York Times, Nov. 15, 1928.
61. Susan Breul, "Words and Music" in The Bridgeport Sunday Post, July 31st, 1938.

er at the Stanford University at Palo Alto, Cal. Alexander Nepritzky-Granowsky is professor of entomology at the University of Minnesota.

Ukrainian S t u n d i sts from North Dakota, German Mennonites and Russian Doukhobory brought with them from Ukraine several varieties of seeds which were adapted to American climate and soil and are now in wide use through the American West and Middle-West. "Kubanka," "Crimean" and "Kharkov" are well known kinds of Ukrainian wheat, used now on American plains. Kherson oats, some Ukrainian kinds of rye, buckwheat, alfalfa, sunflowers and millet are extensively planted by American farmers. [62]

The known song "Don't Forget Me" from the operetta "Song of the Flame" is but a sample of several Ukrainian motives which penetrated into the work of Gershwin and other American composers.

## Statistics

According to the 1930 (fifteenth United States Census, — 58,685 persons of foreign birth listed their mother tongue as Ukrainian and 9,800 as — Ruthenian. [63] Of course, both names denote the same nationality and the official number of American first generation Ukrainians in 1930 may be stated as 68,485.

To this number the "Russians" from Austria, Hungary, Poland, Czechoslovakia and Rumania must be added. There are no Russians in those countries, or so few that the Russian immigration from them could never amount to 41,840 persons, as listed in the Census. Taking into account that some 20% of the 26,797 Polish "Russians" were of White Russian nationality, the rest must be considered with 6,538 "Russians" from Czechoslovakia, 6,310 from Austria, 1,791 from Rumania and 414 from Hungary, either as Ukrainian Russophiles, or those Ukrainians who named their nationality as "Roosin" and were listed as Russians. This would add 36,481 persons to the above official number of Ukrainians and Ruthenians.

Outside of these "Russians" from countries other than Russia, many Ukrainian immigrants from the Russian Empire have been listed as "Rus-

62. D. Borodin, "Russian Contributions to Agriculture in America," in The Guide Book to the Exhibit of Russian Section, New York, America's Making, pp. 28-31; Yaroslav Chyz and Joseph Roucek, "The Russians in the United States," Slavonic Review, XVII, 51, London, April 1939.

63. United States Department of Commerce, Bureau of Census. Fifteenth Census of the United States 1930 Population, Vol. II, Statistics by subjects. Mother Tongue of the Foreign Born White Population. Washington, D. C., 1933.

sians." It is impossible even approximately to determine their number except for the state of North Dakota, where the Ukrainian Protestant immigrants from Russian U k r a i n e are called and were listed as "Russians" and where there are hardly any real Russians in the state. Their number is given by the U. S. Census at 3,003.

Thus we obtain, on the basis of the United States Census, a total of 105,969 Ukrainian immigrants in this country in 1930.

The same U. S. Census states also the number of persons of foreign parentage and of mixed parentage, but only by the state of birth of one or both parents, not by their mother tongue. It can be safely assumed that the number of children of foreign and mixed parentage in the Ukrainian group was the same as the average for all foreign-born groups, if not even greater. The foreign parentage group amounts in the United States generally to 127 per cent of the foreign group. This in the case of Ukrainians would give a number of 134,571 persons.

The mixed parentage group amounted in 1930 to 62.5 per cent of all the foreign born. For Ukrainians it would mean 66,231 persons. Thus on the basis of the United States Census

the number of first and second generation Ukrainians in 1930 may be stated as follows:

Foreign born ................105,969
Foreign parentage ........134,571
Mixed parentage ............ 66,231
                            _____
Total ...........................306,771

It must be born in mind that the above calculation represents only those Ukrainians who were listed as such and those who were registered as Ruthenians and Russians from countries where there is no Russian native population. The number of Ukrainians who were listed under the name of the country of their origin (Poland, Hungary, Russia, Rumania) and of those who were erroneously put down as Slovaks because their language is of Slavonic origin, or even as Lithuanians (as was the case with 1,224 Ukrainians in North Dakota in the Thirteenth U. S. Census of 1910), probably equals if not exceeds the above figure.

Figures obtained through application of the same method to the statistics of the United States Bureau of Immigration are quite different. According to the annual reports of the said bureau for 1899-1930, [64] — 30,284,890 immigrants from Eu-

64. Annual Report of the Commissioner General of Immigration 1931 (United States Department of Labor, Washington, 1931), pp. 216-226.

rope and Canada arrived in the United States. In 1930 the United States Bureau of Census reported 13,366,407 white persons of foreign birth. This number represents 44.1 per cent of all arrivals for thirty-one years previous to that date.

In the same period of years, according to the Immigration Report, — 268,421 Ukrainians (Ruthenians, Russniaks) arrived in this country. Accepting for them the same ratio as for the total of immigration we obtain the number of 129,374 Ukrainians who were alive and present in this country in 1930. Adding the number of persons of foreign and mixed parentage (245,161), obtained in the same manner as used above, we arrive at the figure of 374,535 persons as the estimated number of Ukrainians and their children in the United States in 1930 [65]

According to a very conservative estimate of this author based on federal, fraternal and revised church statistics and on reports on mass meetings, rallies and other manifestations of Ukrainian group life in this country the minimum number of persons of Ukrainian birth and descent in 796 localities, [66] where Ukrainian colonies could be reliably established, must be placed at over 650,000. Their estimated distribution in 1935, for which year most of the necessary data were available, is shown in the following table:

---

65. Other estimates of the number of Ukrainians in America are as follows: In 1892, Rev. K. Andruchovich, op. cit., p. 10, put the number of Ukrainian immigrants at 60,000. In 1899, Rev. K. Bonchevsky, in the weekly Svoboda, No. 7, 1899, estimated that 200,000 immigrants from the Austro-Hungarian part of the Ukrainian territory were living in the United States. In 1909, Julian Bachinsky, op. cit., pp. 86-114, by way of a very ingenious calculation arrived at the conclusion that at that time 470,000 Ukrainian immigrants and their children were present in this country. In 1922, the Inter-Racial Council of New York put the number of persons of Ukrainian birth and descent at 500,000. Jerome Da-

vis, The Russians and Ruthenians in America (New York, 1922), p. ix, estimated in 1922 that the number of Ukrainians was between 400,000 and 600,000. In 1924, Nicholas Ceglinsky, "Ukrainians in America," in The Interpreter, December, 1924, Vol. III, No. 12, pp. 4-7, thought that "five hundred thousand seems to be a fair estimate of the number of Ukrainians in the United States." In 1934, Wasyl Halich, "Economic Aspects of Ukrainian Activity in the United States," University of Iowa Studies, 1934, Vol. X, No. 3, pp. 95-103, propounded that 700,000 was a reasonable number, the figure which was also accepted by the Ukrainian Encyclopedia, published in the same year in Lwiw.

66. Mr. Wasyl Halich in his book Ukrainians in the United States names only 588 localities with "Ukrainian organized groups and larger unorganized groups in 1936." It is evident that he has omitted over 250 localities in the eastern states, mostly those with Carpatho-Russian organizations only. He names instead 59 localities, mostly in the western states (Iowa, Minnesota, North Dakota, Montana, Wisconsin, Wyoming, Texas) with small groups of farmers, often with few families only.

| State | No. of localities with Ukrainian population | No. of churches | No. of fraternal lodges | Membership of churches | Membership of fraternal lodges | Estimated number of Ukrainians |
|---|---|---|---|---|---|---|
| Pennsylvania | 372 | 278 | 1,665 | 179,850 | 108,330 | 230,000 |
| New York | 72 | 68 | 287 | 53,850 | 18,740 | 75,000 |
| New Jersey | 69 | 52 | 250 | 43,700 | 20,740 | 60,000 |
| Ohio | 61 | 47 | 266 | 37,100 | 19,750 | 36,000 |
| Connecticut | 33 | 23 | 92 | 12,800 | 6,000 | 25,000 |
| West Virginia | 29 | 8 | 48 | 5,100 | 2,200 | 10,000 |
| Massachusetts | 26 | 11 | 28 | 3,400 | 1,150 | 15,000 |
| Illinois | 25 | 19 | 110 | 18,150 | 6,750 | 35,000 |
| Michigan | 21 | 14 | 60 | 7,800 | 4,300 | 27,000 |
| Indiana | 11 | 10 | 44 | 6,400 | 2,750 | 12,000 |
| North Dakota | 7 | 15 | | 2,330 | | 11,000 |
| Other States & Dist. of Columb. | 70 | 42 | 166 | 19,020 | 9,850 | 120,000 |
| TOTAL | 796 | 587 | 3,016 | 389,500 | 200,560 | 656,000 |

A very conservative estimate of persons of Ukrainian birth and descent outside of the 796 localities listed in the above table runs between 50 and 100 thousand. **Thus 700,000 can be accepted safely as the minimum number of all American Ukrainians in 1935.**

The largest center of the Ukrainian population* is the soft-coal and foundry region of south-western P e n n s y l v a n i a within the city of Pittsburgh. There, in Allegheny, Washington, Westmoreland, Fayette, Indiana, Cambria and Clearfield

---

\* Larger part of the statistical material for this estimate was collected, tabulated and classified by Mrs. Y. J. Chyz.

counties, 153 out of 372 Ukrainian colonies in Pennsylvania are located. The Ukrainians in that part of the state work in soft-coal mines, in foundries and car factories of the Pittsburgh industrial area. The city of Pittsburgh alone with some 70 fraternal lodges and 15 churches has from fifteen to twenty thousand Ukrainians.

Another area thickly populated by Ukrainians is the hard coal region of Scranton, Wilkes-Barre and Pottsville. Some 98 known colonies are in existence in Lackawanna, Luzerne, Carbon, Schuylkill and Northumberland counties. Men in that region work mostly in anthracite mines, and women in silk mills.

The third center of Ukrainians in Pennsylvania is the city of Philadelphia with five Ukrainian National Homes, nine churches, 70 fraternal lodges and over a score of other organizations. The Ukrainian population of Philadelphia can be estimated at between ten to fifteen thousand.

New York City with around one hundred societies·and fraternal lodges, sixteen religious congregations, three "national homes" and some 30,000 persons of Ukrainian birth and descent has by far the largest group of them in any one city. Ukrainians here have more than a score of professional men and women, and the presence of their best artistic talent makes New York a sort of cultural center of the Ukrainian immigration in America. The immigrants and their children are employed in every industry, a considerable number of them being furriers, tailors, bakery and restaurant workers and window-cleaners. Over a half of Local Number 95 of the House Wreckers Union of New York City are the immigrants from what is now Soviet Ukraine. [67]

Large Ukrainian colonies are in the neighboring towns over the Hudson River, in Jersey City, Passaic, Paterson, Bayonne, the most numerous being in Newark. Some twelve to fifteen thousand Ukrainians live there, organized in about thirty societies and six churches.

Chicago, with about sixty societies and lodges and eleven churches, has close to 25,000 persons of Ukrainian birth and descent. Detroit (including Hamtramck), with more than forty societies and lodges, four National Homes and ten churches, has fifteen to eighteen thousand Ukrainians with most of the men working in the automobile industry.

### Occupations

In all these cities the second and third generations of Ukrainians enter all fields of "gainful occupation" and thousands of them are working as bookkeepers, stenographers, office clerks and in all other professions.

Close to ninety per cent of Ukrainian immigrants are miners and industrial workers. Probably the majority of their children, if occupied, work also in American industries. Some 26,000 of them live on farms. [68] Compact farmers' communities

---

67. See: A. Parry, "Artists of Wrecking," Esquire, April 1936, pp. 92 ff.

68. W. Halich, "Ukrainian Farmers in the United States," Agricultural History, Vol. 10, No. 1, January 1936, pp. 25-39.

are found in North Dakota (Kiev, Russo, Max, Butte, Ukraina, Gorham). Other communities are found around Syracuse, Albany and Saratoga, N. Y.; Colchester, Conn.; Holyoke and Deerfield, Massachusetts; Harrah, Oklahoma; Clayton, Wisconsin; with scattered small groups of f a r m e r s throughout New Jersey (Nova Ukraina), Ohio, Michigan, Pennsylvania, Indiana and even Texas.

The Ukrainian professional class, including the clergy, hardly amounts to one-half of one per cent of the total of Ukrainian immigration, and has not yet made itself so conspicuous in American life as corresponding classes of older immigrant groups, although it is g r o w i n g constantly. Several thousand Ukrainians serve their communities as grocers, butchers, undertakers, tailors, with few of them active in other fields of business on a bigger scale.

In conclusion of this outline I want to express my appreciation to Prof. Joseph S. Roucek, Hofstra College, with whom I have prepared an article on Ukrainians in America a few years ago. [69] The experience gained

from him at that time and some of the material we collected for the other article have been of great help to me now. [70]

---

69. Y. Chyz and J. S. Roucek, "American Ukrainians" in Our Racial and National Minorities, Prentice Hall, New York, 1937.

70. For additional works on Ukrainian immigrants in America in English besides those mentioned in references see the following:

Samuel McLanahan, Our People of Foreign Speech, Fleming H. Revell Company, New York, Chicago, Toronto, 1904, pp. 54-55.

I. Ardan, "Ruthenians in the United States," Charities and Commons, Dec. 3, 1904, XIII; 246-252.

T. Roberts, "The Slavs in the Anthracite Coal Communities," Ibid, pp. 215-222.

Emily G. Balch, "A Shepherd of Immigrants," Ibid., pp. 193-194.

Lillian Shrewsbury Mesick, "Galician Failure and One Christmas Tree," Paradise of Pacific, Honolulu, Hawaii, January, 1912: 33-39.

Emily G. Balch, Our Slavic Fellow Citizens, Charities Publishing Committee, New York, 1919, passim, esp. Chapt. VII, pp. 120-147.

Jerome Davis, The Russians and Ruthenians in America, Doran, New York, 1922.

Nicholas Ceglinsky, "Ukrainians in America," Our World, Dec. 1924, IV: 85-88. "The Ukrainian Immigrant; His Group Interests," Interpreter, 1923, No. 3, II: 3-6; "Ukrainian Community Centers," Ibid., No. 12, p. 15; "How the Ukrainians Came," Ibid., 1924, No. 1, III, pp. 5-7; "Ukrainians in America," Ibid., No. 12, III, pp. 4-7.

A. H. Eton, The Immigrant Gifts to American Life, Russel Sage Foundation, New York, 1932, passim.

H. G. Duncan, Immigration and Assimilation, D. C. Heath, Boston, 1933, Chapt. XVII, pp. 252-278, 764-770.

Marie S. Gambal, Our Ukrainian Background, Ukrainian Workingmen's Association, Scranton, Pa., 1936.

Wasyl Halich, "Ukrainians in Western Pennsylvania," The Western Pennsylvania Historical Magazine (Pittsburgh, June 1935), Vol. 18, 2, pp. 139-146.

**Yaroslav J. Chyz**

UKRAINIAN DAYS IN NEW YORK STATE
AND NEW YORK CITY
1955

At the beginning of 1955, the days of January 22, 1955 and January 23, 1955 were proclaimed as Ukrainian Days by Governor Averell Harriman of New York State, and Mayor Robert Wagner of New York City. The following are the texts of the proclamations.

PROCLAMATION
STATE OF NEW YORK
Executive Chamber

Thirty-seven years ago on January 22nd, the free and independent Ukrainian Republic was proclaimed. Ukrainians and those of Ukrainian descent all over the world will observe this anniversary as an occasion to reassert their belief in freedom and to reaffirm their conviction that when men so believe tyranny and despotism cannot long prevail.

The fall of the Ukrainian National Republic did not dim the spirit which brought it to life. The love of freedom still reigns in the hearts of the Ukrainian people and sustains them in their opposition to the heavy-handed rule of communist tyranny. Here in America their efforts have served to strengthen our purpose and our resolve to resist this evil wherever it appears.

The people of New York welcome the opportunity to honor a freedom-loving people by joining in the observance of this anniversary.

NOW, THEREFORE, I, Averell Harriman, Governor of the State of New York, do proclaim Saturday, January 22, 1955, as
UKRAINIAN DAY
in the State of New York, and call upon the people of the State of New York to join with their fellow citizens of Ukrainian descent in the hope and prayer that peace, freedom and justice may be restored to a brave people now held in bondage to communist tyranny.

Given under my hand and the Privy Seal of the State at the Capitol in the City of Albany this seventeenth day of January in the year of our Lord One thousand nine hundred and fifty-five.

BY THE GOVERNOR

Averell Harriman (signed)

## Office of the Mayor
### CITY OF NEW YORK

# Proclamation

**WHEREAS:** January 22, 1955, will mark the thirty-seventh Anniversary of the proclamation of a free and independent Ukrainian Republic, and those of Ukranian origin, all over the world, will celebrate this date as a memorial to the once free people, and

**WHEREAS** the love of freedom and democracy still lives in the hearts of the men and women of the Ukraine despite Communistic oppression, and their matchless faith and courage will always defeat the aggressor seeking their ultimate enslavement, and

**WHEREAS** our citizens of Ukranian origin, who enjoy the privilegs of our great nation, while striving for the ultimate release of the enslaved men, women and children in the homeland, will especially mark the day dedicated to Ukranian democracy.

NOW, THEREFORE, I, Robert F. Wagner, Mayor of The City of New York, do hereby proclaim Sunday, January 23, 1955, as
### UKRANIAN DAY
in New York City, and call upon all our citizens to join with those of Ukranian origin in prayers for peace, freedom and justice in the world.

IN WITNESS WHEREOF I have hereunto set my hand and caused the SEAL of The City of New York to be affixed this 17th day of January, 1955.

Robert F. Wagner (signed)
Mayor, The City of New York

## UKRAINIAN AMERICAN ORGANIZATIONS
## IN NEW YORK CITY
## 1955

Dr. Alexander Sokolyshyn, a noted Ukrainian researcher, author, and bibliographer
on Ukrainian topics, devoted one of his
studies to organized Ukrainian American
life in New York City. A substantial part
of the study is reproduced below.

Source: Ukrainian Congress Committee.
Golden Jubilee Book Commemorating Organized American Life in New York: 1905-
1955. New York, 1955.

It is difficult to state the exact date of the first settlement of Ukrainian
immigrants in the new world, or in the world's greatest metropolis,
New York. Historians of Ukrainian immigrants in the United States
claim that one of the first Ukrainian immigrants in New York was the
famous Albridt Zaborowskyj, in all probability a Ukrainian exile from
Poland who arrived to New York in 1662. There is also evidence that
the adjutant to General George Washington, Tadej Kostjushko was
a Ukrainian. Then there is the brother of the well known Ukrainian writer and priest Marijan Shashkewytch, who came to New York in the
beginning of the 19th century. He is considered as among the first
settlers of Ukrainian immigrants in the metropolitan area. There was
Petro Sokalskyj, the Ukrainian composer of symphony music and opera
Taras Bulba; he was employed by the Russian consulate in New York
in the 1860's. In 1865, ninety years ago, Rev. Agapius Honcharenko
arrived to New York having escaped from Russia for his revolutionary
activities. He is considered as one of the first educated Ukrainians in
America, later he became editor of the Alaska Herald which was published
in San Francisco, California, in the Russian, Ukrainian and English
languages for the people of Alaska.

However, the major wave of Ukrainian immigrants in the New
York Metropolitan area, date back to the second half of the 19th century.
At first, Ukrainian activities centered around churches, developing sub-
sequently into fraternal organizations, choirs, dramatic clubs and some
publishing enterprises. One of the first pioneers was Rev. Ivan Voljansky,
appointed in 1884 by the Metropolitan of Lwiw, Sylvester Cardinal Sem-
bratovych, parish priest of U. S. A. One of the earliest societies in New
York was the women's organization "Sisterhood of Saint Olga" established
in 1897 and active until 1907. Another early Ukrainian society in New
York was the "Brotherhood of Nicholas", which entered the U. N. A.

formation in 1899. Further, "Zorja" was established in 1901, the society "Zaporiska Sich" was formed in 1903. In 1904 "St. Andrew's Brotherhood" was established and the U. N. A. Branch 130 of St. Volodymyr, which is still active today. The first Greek Catholic parish was established in 1905 on 20th Street and transferred to East 7th Street in 1911.

In 1905 a meeting was called by Peter Jarema on behalf of Zorja and Zaporiska Sich societies in New York City. The purpose of this meeting was to create one strong representative United Ukrainian Organizations Committee, comprised from the various Ukrainian societies in New York, in order to coordinate their activities. Thus begun the Ukrainian organized civic life in New York City. This occasion is being commemorated by the publication of the first Souvenir Book on the Golden Anniversary of the United Ukrainian American Organizations Committee. This meeting was attended by more than 200 members of "Zorja", "Zaporiska Sich", "I. Naumowitch" and the "St. Vladimir" societies. In 1905 the first meeting of the Ukrainian women was called for the express purpose of building and finding homes for the arriving immigrants in New York City. By 1907 there were twelve Ukrainian American societies.

A cultural society "Prosvita" was established in New York in 1908 and it is also still active after giving much aid to the Old Country during the time of its existence. "Free Cossacks of the City of Lwiw" was founded in 1912 and "Freedom in America" which merged in 1926 with the 172nd U. N. A. Branch into Branch 361 of U. N. A. "Dnister". In 1912 "Providence Association" composed of Ukrainian Catholics in U. S. A. was formed and "Bukovyna" Association was founded in 1915 uniting immigrants from Bukovyna. With the outbreak of World War I activities of Ukrainians in New York assumed a faster tempo, all societies hurrying to the aid of their former homeland now engulfed by the war. In 1914 the "Ukrajinska Rada" united the Ukrainian organizations in New York. 1915 was the beginning of political action, like e. g. a Protest Meeting against Russian imprisonment of Professor Mychajlo Hrushevsky, and the "First Ukrainian Assembly" which was to be the Ukrainian representative political body in the United States.

There were about 50 Ukrainian organizations in New York by 1915, and on November 18th they joined in establishing "Ukrainska Narodna Hromada" (Ukrainian National Community) which united 44 societies and was chartered on March 30, 1916. This organization purchased a Ukrainian National Home on May 19, 1916 on East 6th St. for $ 46,500.00, Rev. Mykola Pidhoretsky became president and Mr. Peter Zadoretsky secretary. The organization took active part in the "Ukrainian Day" proclaimed in 1917 by President Woodrow Wilson at the request of Ukrainians. The period immediately following the war, after Ukraine's unsuccessful fight for independence, brought a wave of immigration to the United States, particularly of former Ukrainian political and military leaders. The "Ukrainian Youth Association" was founded in 1921 and became quite active. In 1922 the "League of Ukrainian American Citizens" and in 1924 the "Ukrainian American Federation Committee" Branch New York was formed and became active. By 1925 there was an "Association of Ukrainian National Societies" in the City of New York, headed by Mychajlo Nykyforchyn. On the initiative of the late Maria Skubova, Ukrainian women's societies were reactivated, notably "Ukrainska Zhinocha Hromada" (1921) and "Tovarystvo Ukrainska Zhinocha Pomich" (1925). The well-known Ukrainian women's organization which is active to this day, "Soyuz Ukrainok Ameryky" was established in 1925 as well as U. N. A. Branch 204.

The Ukrainian Orthodox parish and church of St. Vladimir was established in its present E. 14 Street location in 1926. In 1930 the Central Committee of Ukrainian National Organizations in New York was established.

One of the most impressive manifestations of the Ukrainian community in New York was the Protest March and Demonstration of November 15, 1930 against Polish pacification of West Ukraine. According to press reports, 82 organizations with 20,000 people took part in this demonstration which ended in front of the Polish consulate. Other notable events in New York were: the appearance of "Ballet School of Avramenko" in the Metropolitan Opera in 1931 with 1000 dancers; demonstration against the organization of a famine in Ukraine by the U. S. S. R. in 1933 and against American recognition of the Soviet government. In 1935 there was a concert in honor of Shevchenko in Town Hall, conducted by the composer O. Koshets. In 1936 a concert in honor of Metropolitan Sheptytsky was given in Carnegie Hall. Ukrainians took part in the N. Y. World's Fair in 1939; Ukrainian women also exhibited their embroideries in New York. When Hungary occupied Carpatho-Ukraine in 1939 the Ukrainians of New York staged a Manifestation in protest.

During the period between the wars, an important role was played by ODVU (Society for rebirth of Ukraine) established in 1929 on the advice of Col. E. Konovalets, Branches of U. N. A. and Sich. Central Ukrainian organizations at this time were: "Ukrainian League of American Citizens", "Committee of United UNA Branches", "Central Committee of Ukrainian American Organizations in the City of New York." In 1930 the Ukrainian organizations in New York gave the initiative towards the establishment of the supreme Ukrainian political body in the United States, the Ukrainian Congress Committee, which took place in December, 1939 at the Congress of Ukrainian Centers in the U. S. A., i. e. United Ukrainian Organizations, active from 1922 to 1940. The Congress of Ukrainians in America was held in Washington, D. C. on May 24, 1940 with partipation of 805 delegates, and it established the UCCA whose representation in New York is carried out by the Committee of Ukrainian

American Organizations in the City of New York. The Committee was first established on December 15, 1942 on the initiative of a Committee of U. N. A. branches and with participation of delegates from 35 organizations. At the meeting Mr. Dmytro Halychyn (president of U. N. A. and U. C. C. A.) presided. The Committee elected Mr. S. Kowalchuk its chairman, and Mr. Maletych secretary, the author of its by-laws was Mr. Eugene Lachovych, which provided for coordination of societies in New York and aid to Ukraine. The by-laws also provided for wartime aid to the United States and the Committee transferred money collected at various affairs organized by it to the American Red Cross. Ukrainian radio programs cooperated with the Committee. The Committee sent its delegates to the various Ukrainian conventions and forwarded resolutions demanding of the United States government recognition of Ukraine's independence. In 1944 the Committee elected M. Havrylko, Esq. chairman and Messrs. M. Maletych and P. Kuchma secretary and treasurer respectively, and they are carrying out these duties with devotion to this day. The Committee helped celebrate the 50th Anniversary of the UNA, the Ukrainian American Veterans to erect two monuments in N. Y. (Tompkins Park and 2nd Ave.) honoring Ukrainian soldiers killed in service of the U. S. A. etc. The Committee's liason with the UCCA was maintained by Mr. D. Halychyn. The Committee also aided in the acquisition of the Ukrainian National Home in New York.

While during the war the Committee devoted much time and work to promoting bond drives and taking part in all major tasks confronting Americans of Ukrainian origin in the United States, that of aiding their Ukrainian brethren in resisting forcible repatriation to the U. S. S. R. and helping them to migrate to the U. S. and other free lands of the Western World became of prime importance after the war. The Committee actively participated in the work of the UUARC and its director, Dr. Walter Gallan and contributed not only funds, but also much work of its members.

In 1949 the Committee and its member organizations took part in the Loyalty Parade in New York City under the command of Walter Bacad, commander of Ukrainian American Veterans, and have continued to take part in this parade ever since.

In 1950 the Committee took part in the Spring Festival of American Youth at Carnegie Hall and in the 10th Anniversary of the founding of the Ukrainian Congress Committee which was participated in by both New York Senators Ives and Lehman, Prof. James Burnham and the Hon. Dikur, Ukrainian deputy in the Canadian Federal Parliament. In November 1950 the Committee held a commemorative evening in honor of the commander-in-chief of the Ukrainian Insurgent Army, General Taras Chuprynka who was killed in action by the communists earlier that year. The period of 1949 to 1951 was one of the Committee's greatest activity and the guiding idea was to give moral and material aid to fighting Ukrainian forces embodied in such organizations as OUN, UPA and UHVR, so as to popularize the Ukrainian problem in the free world. An anti-Moscow demonstration was held in Manhattan Center in 1951, and wide support was given to the resolution of Congressman Kersten which called for aid to nations enslaved by Moscow. The annual meeting of 1952 was conducted under the chairmanship of the Hon. Julian Revaj, former Prime Minister of Carpatho-Ukraine, and the meeting in recognition of M. Havrylko, Esq. having been President of the Committee for 10 consecutive years, elected him Honorary President. Many commemorative and patriotic affairs were held during the years 1952, 1953, 1954 and 1955 like picketing the Soviet farmers and the 10th U. N. General Assembly meeting.

Early in 1954 the Committee sponsored the publication of a book to commemorate the 10th Anniversary of the Ukrainian Insurgent Army, under the title "Ukrainian Insurgent Army in Fight for Freedom".

A sum of $ 3286.73 was donated by various organizations toward this book. This book has been distributed to the various libraries throughout the United States.

A protest demonstration was held on the 20th of March in 1954 on the anniversary of the great Famine and genocide in Ukraine committed by Moscow. The demonstration was widely reported in the American press. The Committee also actively supported Rep. Lawrence Smith's House Resolution No. 58 calling for the establishment of direct diplomatic relations between the United States of America on the one, and the Republic of Ukraine and Byelorussia on the other. The Committee protested to the United Nations, the U. S. Government and the Dominion of Canada and Australia against the forcible repatriation of the Ukrainian seaman Ostrokov to the Soviet Union, who committed suicide in Italy while on his way of being deported to the land of communism. Mrs. Eleonor Roosevelt joined in this Committee's efforts to explain to the world the circumstances of this tragic case. The Committee also engaged in gathering signatures in protest against the admission of Communist China to the United Nations, and took part in greeting the five Chinese who refused to be repatriated in Town Hall in the summer of 1954.

In the summer of 1954 the Committee demonstrated against the Soviet celebrations of the 300th anniversary of the Ukrainian-Russian Treaty of Alliance of Pereyaslav at which Governor Averell Harriman was one of the chief speakers. Due to the efforts of the Committee, the Governor of New York, Averell Harriman proclaimed on January 21, 1955 and Mayor Robert F. Wagner of New York on January 23, 1955 — a UKRAINIAN DAY in the presence of Ukrainian delegations headed by Stephen Jarema, Esq. and Committee Chairman Peter Kuchma. On this occasion, for the first time in the history of the City of New York, the Ukrainian Flag flew above City Hall.

The Ukrainian flag was presented to the City by our Committee a branch of the Ukrainian Congress Committee.

On June 28th, 1955 the representatives of the Ukrainian American organizations participated in the National Unity Day in New York City with Ukrainian national costumes and the Ukrainian national flag. The event was held at the Statue of Liberty commemorating Bedloe Island's transformation to a national shrine honoring all the immigrants. This shrine will be known as the Museum of Immigrants.

With the demolition of the Third Avenue El, the Ukrainians were one of the 45 nationality groups who took part in the ceremonies on August 1st, 1955. The Ukrainians were greeted by Boro President Jack Hulan on the East 6th Street corner and Third Avenue.

Last but not least where the Ukrainians partook in a public affair was the 10th Anniversary of the United Nations, whereby they were present at the Mayor's reception in City Hall, New York.

## UKRAINIAN AMERICAN YOUTH ACTIVITY
## IN NEW YORK CITY
## 1955

A brief article on the Ukrainian American
youth movement, its activities, and achievements was written by Stephen Shumeyko.  The
article is entirely reproduced.

Source:  Ukrainian Congress Committee.
Golden Jubilee Book Commemorating Organized
American Life in New York:  1905-1955.  New
York, 1955.

The Ukrainian American Youth Movement, as it is called, dates way
back to early 1920's. In those days, here in New York City, there was a
group of Ukrainian students and professionals, which used to meet
regularly and which published a periodical of its own. Among its members
were Dr. Nelie Pelechovich, Dr. George Andreyko, Mr. Wladimir Semenu-
na noted translator of Ukrainian poetry, and an engineer by profession, and
Mr. Stephen Schumeyko, then a college student.

At that time there existed the United Ukrainian Organiztion of the United
States ("Obyednanye"), the president of which was Mr. Emil Revyuk, secretary the late Dr. Luke Myshuha, treasurer, Mr. Dmytro Halychyn. Every
year that organization, which was nationally representative, held its annual
meetings. At each of these meetings, the Ukrainian American youth problem
was one of the principal items on the agenda. All aspects of it were presented and discussed by the American born Ukrainian youth.

In concurrence with this quite a number of our young persons from the
New York Metropolitan Area and from elsewhere as well, including Philadelphia, Newark, and Chicago, began to write for the "Svoboda" in English.
Their reports were reports about their community affairs, comments on their
Ukrainian American life in general, essays, translations of Ukrainian poetry
by Mr. Semenyna, and a "Short History of Ukraine" by Mr. Shumeyko
which ran serially for about one year.

In 1933, the idea was conceived to convene a Ukrainian Youth's Congress of America. It was held in Chicago, in August, during the Chicago
World's Fair, throughout the Ukrainian Week. It resulted in the establishment of the Ukrainian Youth's League of North America, non-partisan and
non-sectarian in nature, and devoted to American principles and to the Ukrainian Cause

Since then the Ukrainian Youth's League of North America has been
a great unifying force in Ukrainian American youth life. It has held yearly
conventions in Eastern and Mid-West cities, which have been attended by
delegates of various youth societies, cultural, social and athletic, the forma-

tion of which it helped to inspire and promote.

The League conventions, which were very well attended year after year except during World War II,featured, aside from the social events, serious discussions during the open Forum sessions in the course of which matters and issues pertaining to Ukrainian American life, as well as how the youth could best help the Ukrainian people in their native albeit enslaved Ukraine regain their national freedom and independence.

In all this, of course, The Ukrainian Weekly, English supplement of the "Svoboda" daily, published by the Ukrainian National Association, a fraternal benefit order, founded back in 1894, played a very important part in the matter of publicity and in editorially suggesting and encouraging ideas for the Ukrainian American youth to follow.

Ukrainian American youth manifestations, held under the auspices of the Ukrainian Youth's League of North America, and helped by the publicity of the "Svoboda" and the Ukrainian Weekly, and the persons associated with it, included a concert and dance exhibition held in Cleveland,Ohio in 1937, and at the World's Fair Exposiotion held in New York in 1941. More than 20,000 persons witnessed the Ukrainian show at the latter.

One of the attractions at this and other programs was the Ukrainian Youth Chorus of New York and New Jersey, directed by Mr.Stephen Marusevich and organized by this writer. This chorus also sang on nation-wide hook-ups over the radio, such as the National Broadcasting Company, on Labor Day, from Pittsburg, the same network out of New York, in 1940, and the Mutual Broadcasting System, WOR, out of Newark in September, 1939. The latter program, incidentally, was interruped near its end by the annoucement that World War II had began.

In time that chorus re-organized itself, and under the auspices of the Ukrainian American Youth Committee of the New York Metropolitan Area presented a number of fine concerts. Its greatest feat was its "Echoes of Ukraine", presented at Carnegie Hall, New York.

Worth noting, too, its that the Ukrainian American youth of the N.Y.-N. J. area played a great role in the success of the mass chorus over 300 singers known as the"Simka." It was first directed by the late Hayvoronsky, and after that by Koshetz. The Carnegie and Town Hall concerts, conducted by Koshetz, were something out of this world. But what especially important was the preparation that went into these concerts. Every Sunday afternoon during the summer time, the young choristers would sacrifice a trip to the beach or to the mountains, and from New York, Newark, Yonkers, Jersey City, Elizabeth, Perth Amboy, Brooklyn, and elswhere, they would regularly arrive, by car or bus, led by their choir conductors as Mr. Theodosius Kaskiw of Newark, and in the sweltering heat go over and over again the songs under the inspired direction of Koshetz.

Ukrainian American youth activity in these days is definitely on the-bound. The dance group led by Mr. Walter Bacad and Mr. Flis as well as by

Mr. William Polewchak is definitely superior in choreography and training to those of the past. Their performances on TV have helped a good deal to acquait many with this particular aspect of Ukrainian culture.

These comments, it should be noted, are only marginal. A much longer article, and, for that matter, a book could and should be written about Ukrainian American youth life during the past several decades not only in the New York Metropolitan Area but throughout the country as well, in all of its entirety. It would make interesting and instructive reading.

## PRESIDENT DWIGHT D. EISENHOWER
## GREETS UKRAINIAN AMERICANS
## 1955

On December 15, 1955, President Dwight
D. Eisenhower sent the following telegram to the Ukrainian American Organizations Committee of New York.

Source:  Ukrainian Congress Committee.
<u>Golden Jubilee Book Commemorating Or-
ganized American Life in New York</u>: 1905-
1955. New York, 1955.

**WESTERN UNION**
**TELEGRAM**

CLASS OF SERVICE

This is a fast message unless its deferred char-acter is indicated by the proper symbol.

SYMBOLS

DL = Day Letter
NL = Night Letter
LT = International Letter Telegram

1201

W. P. MARSHALL, President

The filing time shown in the date line on domestic telegrams is STANDARD TIME at point of origin. Time of receipt is STANDARD TIME at point of destination

sPA902                                   1955 DEC 15  PM 3 37

P GLA 062 Long GOVT NL PD — GETTYSBURG PENN 15 —
PETER KUCHMA, President —

UNITED AMERICAN UKRAINIAN ORGANIZATIONS COMMIT-
TEE OF NEW YORK UKRAINIAN CONGRESS COMMITTEE OF
AMERICA, Inc. 140-142 SECOND AVE NYC —

To the Members of the United Ukrainian American Organizations
in New York I extend warm Greetings on the occasion of the Fiftieth
Anniversary of the founding of their organization.

Such fraternal organizations are an important part of our democratic
Society. They play a significant role in promoting mutual understanding
among the widely diversified groups that make up the American community. Please accept this expression of my appreciation of your organization's efforts to combat international Communism and to instill
a high sense of civic responsibility among Americans of Ukrainian
descent —

## DWIGHT D. EISENHOWER

TARAS SHEVCHENKO STATUE
IN WASHINGTON, D. C.
1960

On September 13, 1960, Public Law 86-749
authorized the erection of a statue of
Taras Shevchenko, a great Ukrainian poet
and fighter for freedom. Here is the
text of the law.

Source: U.S. Statutes at Large 86-2,
1960, vol. 74 (Public Laws).

## SHEVCHENKO STATUE

### PUBLIC LAW 86–749; 74 STAT. 884

[H. J. Res. 311]

Joint Resolution authorizing the erection of a statue of Taras Shevchenko on public grounds in the District of Columbia.

WHEREAS throughout Eastern Europe, in the last century and this, the name and works of Taras Shevchenko brilliantly reflected the aspirations of man for personal liberty and national independence; and

WHEREAS Shevchenko, the poet laureat of Ukraine, was openly inspired by our great American tradition to fight against the imperialist and colonial occupation of his native land; and

WHEREAS in many parts of the free world observances of the Shevchenko centennial will be held during 1961 in honor of this immortal champion of liberty; and

WHEREAS in our moral capacity as free men in an independent Nation it behooves us to symbolize tangibly the inseparable spiritual ties bound in the writings of Shevchenko between our country and the forty million Ukrainian nation: Now, therefore, be it

*Resolved by the Senate and House of Representatives of the United States of America in Congress assembled, That:*

(a) Any association or committee organized for such purpose within two years from the date of the enactment of this joint resolution is hereby authorized to place on land owned by the United States in the District of Columbia a statue of the Ukrainian poet and national leader, Taras Shevchenko.

(b) The authority granted by subsection (a) of this section shall cease to exist, unless within five years after the date of enactment of this joint resolution (1) the erection of the statue is begun, and (2) the association or committee certifies to the Secretary of the Interior the amount of funds available for the purpose of the completion of the statue and the Secretary determines that such funds are adequate for such purpose.

Sec. 2. The Secretary of the Interior is authorized and directed to select an appropriate site upon which to erect the statue authorized in the first section. The choice of the site and the design and plans for such statue shall be subject to the approval of the Commission on Fine Arts and the National Capital Planning Commission. Such statue shall be erected without expense to the United States.

Approved September 13, 1960.

# TARAS SHEVCHENKO FREEDOM LIBRARY
## 1964

The following is the text of a proposed resolution favoring the establishing of the Taras Shevchenko Freedom Library as a section of the Library of Congress.

Source: Shevchenko: A Monument to the Liberation, Freedom, and Independence of All Captive Nations. Washington, D. C.: U. S. Government Printing Office, 1964.

### RESOLUTION FOR A SHEVCHENKO FREEDOM LIBRARY

Mr. Speaker, in view of the growing and intense interest in the works of Shevchenko and the universal significance of the poet himself, we can perform a most valuable educational service in the national interest by establishing in the Library of Congress a section to be known as the Shevchenko Freedom Library. This section would contain all the essential works devoted to the struggles and aspirations of Shevchenko's Ukraine and other captive non-Russian nations for freedom and independence. Such a concentrated library would greatly satisfy and advance the interest and knowledge of all Americans who have been inspired by what has developed since Congress authorized the statue in 1960; it would be a treasure of literary riches that base the President's own observation on Shevchenko:

His work is a noble part of our historical heritage.

For these purposes and in our national interest—which is the interest of world freedom—I submit this joint resolution to establish a section to be known as the Shevchenko Freedom Library in the Library of Congress:

#### H.J. RES. —

Whereas in March 1961, President Kennedy declared: "I am pleased to add my voice to those honoring the great Ukrainian Poet Taras Shevchenko. We honor him for his rich contribution to the culture not only of Ukraine, which he loved so well and described so eloquently, but of the world. His work is a noble part of our historical heritage"; and

Whereas in March 1963, the President paid fitting tribute to the world-renowned Shevchenko Scientific Society in these words: "My congratulations on the 90th anniversary of the Shevchenko Scientific Society, and on your sustained program for support for distinguished scholarship. Among your members have been some of the great names in learning to whom the world owes an incalculable debt. May you continue to extend the frontiers of human knowledge in the years ahead"; and

Whereas in September 1960, President Eisenhower approved and signed a resolution of Congress providing for the establishment of a lasting memorial to Shevchenko's works in behalf of world freedom and justice; and

Whereas, with understanding and vision, the Eighty-sixth Congress of the United States honored this outstanding freedom light by authorizing the erection of a Shevchenko statue on public grounds in the District of Columbia; and

Whereas the initiative of Congress successfully nullified the exploitation of Shevchenko as an historic symbol by both Moscow and its colonial puppets, and the vehement attacks of the latter against these farseeing acts have clearly proven the wisdom of the United States Government in properly claiming Shevchenko as a towering beacon in the march of freedom; and

Whereas for our times and struggles the universal significance of this revered poet and national hero was permanently established in a galaxy punctuated by other luminaries of freedom, such as his contemporaries Abraham Lincoln, the Italian Mazzini, the Pole Mickiewicz, the Hungarian Petöfi and others from different nations and soils; and

Whereas for our time and beyond the supreme importance of Shevchenko's works rests in his early and heroic opposition to traditional Russian imperio-colonialism and in his courageous advocacy of the freedom of all captive nations in the Russian Empire, including the freedom of Jews and all peoples in bondage of suppression and slavery; and

Whereas our expanding American interest in the classic contributions of Shevchenko and their universal import can only receive full educational satisfaction by an accessible concentration of his voluminous works and all related studies at a facility of national convenience: Now, therefore, be it

Resolved by the Senate and House of Representatives of the United States of America in Congress assembled, That a section in the

Library of Congress be established and appropriately designated as the Shevchenko Freedom Library. This library section shall contain all the works written by Taras Shevchenko, both in the original and translations, and all volumes related to his immortal contributions and contents therein. The establishment of this section shall be effected with the expert cooperation of the Shevchenko Scientific Society. Appropriations shall be made for the accomplishment of these purposes.

## UKRAINIAN DAYS PROCLAIMED IN PENNSYLVANIA
## 1964

January 22, 1964 was proclaimed Ukrainian
Day by Governor William Scranton of Pennsyl-
vania, and Mayor James Tate of Philadelphia.
The text of the proclamations follows.

Source: Ukrainian Congress Committee of
America. Ukrainian Independence - January
22, 1918 - Historical Background. New York:
1974.

# CITY OF PHILADELPHIA

# Proclamation

## Whereas...

A new nation, dedicated to the principle that all men are equal and with
liberty for all, was born 46 years ago on January 22, 1918, unifying all
Ukrainian territories into one independent republic; and

Three years later, the Ukrainian National Republic once more was enslaved by the atheistic forces of communism, which now threatens all
God-fearing and freedom-loving people of the world; and

Ukrainian-Americans have been in the forefront in the battle to stem
this terrible tide, which already has engulfed millions throughout Europe
and Asia;

## Now, Therefore...

I, James H. J. Tate, Mayor of the City of Philadelphia, do hereby proclaim,
Wednesday, January 22, 1964, as

### UKRAINIAN INDEPENDENCE DAY

in Philadelphia, and urge our citizens to join with all Ukrainians in appropriately celebrating this observance.

*James H. J. Tate*

MAYOR

*Fredic R. Mann*

CITY REPRESENTATIVE

Given under my hand and the Seal
of the City of Philadelphia this
fourteenth day of January, one thousand nine hundred and sixty-four.

IN THE NAME AND BY AUTHORITY OF THE

COMMONWEALTH OF PENNSYLVANIA
GOVERNOR'S OFFICE
HARRISBURG

PROCLAMATION

UKRAINIAN NATIONAL INDEPENDENCE DAY - JANUARY 22, 1964

WHEREAS,   Forty-five years ago, on January 22, 1918, the Ukrainian
           people, constituting the largest non-Russian nation in
           Eastern Europe, chose to become an independent national
           state; and

WHEREAS,   Only two years later, in 1920, the Ukrainian National
           Republic became one of the first victims of
           imperio-colonialism by the Soviet Union; and

WHEREAS,   The brave people of the Ukraine still bear the oppression
           of tyranny and remain imprisoned behind the Iron
           Curtain; and

WHEREAS,   Many Pennsylvanians proudly trace their ancestry to
           Ukrainian roots and fervently hope and pray for the
           eventual liberation of their fatherland; and

WHEREAS,   All Pennsylvanians are happy to join their neighbors of
           Ukrainian descent in tribute to the brave Ukrainian
           patriots of 1918 and of 1964:

NOW, THEREFORE, I, William W. Scranton, Governor of the
           Commonwealth of Pennsylvania, do hereby proclaim
           January 22, 1964 UKRAINIAN NATIONAL INDEPENDENCE DAY
           in the Commonwealth.

                        GIVEN under my hand and the Great
                        Seal of the State, at the City
                        of Harrisburg, this sixteenth
                        day of January, in the year of
                        our Lord one thousand nine
                        hundred and sixty-four, and of
                        the Commonwealth the one hundred
                        and eighty-eighth.


                        WILLIAM W. SCRANTON
                        GOVERNOR

BY THE GOVERNOR:


Secretary of the Commonwealth

## THE UKRAINIAN CATHOLIC CHURCH IN AMERICA
## 1967

The greatest part of Ukrainian Americans
are of Catholic (Eastern Rite) faith. A
very interesting article dealing with the
activities of the Ukrainian American Catholic Church during World War I was published by Bohdan Procko. The article is
entirely reproduced.

Source: The Ukrainian Quarterly, vol.
XXII, no. 2 (Summer 1967).

With the outbreak of the First World War, for the first time
the Ukrainians in the United States found themselves in a position
of leadership in the affairs of their people as a whole. In the case
of the Ukrainian Catholic Church, the Most Reverend Stephen Ortynsky, bishop for the Ukrainians originating from Austrian Galicia, as
well as for the Rusyns from Hungary's Transcarpathia, felt that the
immigrants must take the lead in the affairs of their kinsmen in
Europe, at least until that time when those in their native land could
act in their own behalf.

He activated, therefore, a general collection of funds to aid
the victims of war, and he was primarily responsible for the organization of the Ruthenian National *Rada* (Council) at a gathering of
delegates from Galician and Transcarpathian parishes held in Philadelphia on December 8, 1914. The Council was to coordinate the efforts of all the Ukrainian and Rusyn Catholic organizations in behalf of their suffering people in Europe.

The hard work, together with the endless difficulties and opposition he encountered, strained the Bishop's nerves and undermined
his health to the extent that he died on March 24, 1916; not, however, before thousands of dollars, as well as considerable quantities of
medical supplies and gift packages, were sent by the Bishop's Or-
dinariat to help relieve the plight of Ukrainian war victims.[1]

Following the death of Bishop Ortynsky, the Papacy appointed
two separate administrators, one for the Ukrainians, the other for
the Rusyns. Because this article is limited to the humanitarian and
patriotic efforts of the American Ukrainian Catholic Church, our
attention will be focused exclusively on the administration of Very

---

* This article is based on a section of a general study on the Ukrainian
Catholic Church in the United States soon to be published.

[1] See Bishop Ortynsky's official diocesan bulletin, *Eparkhiialny Vistnyk*,
II (May 24, 1915), 3; III (March 8, 1916), 9-10.

Reverend Peter Poniatishin. Since his administration (1916-1924) encompassed the years during which the Ukrainian problem came to the fore, Father Poniatishin did not shirk what he felt was his responsibility. Consequently, the Church played a leading role in this important national and humanitarian work during those critical years.

On Nov. 1, 1916, a committee of the Ukrainian clergy met with delegates from the Ukrainian National Assn. (*Soyuz*), Providence Assn., and "Zhoda Bratstv" and organized the Ukrainian National Alliance.[2] It must be noted here, that, upon becoming the administrator of the Ukrainian part of the diocese, Father Poniatishin took practical steps to end successfully the misunderstanding that existed between the Church and the *Soyuz* since 1910.[3] The renewed friendly relations between the Church and *Soyuz* had excellent results in the humanitarian and political work of the American Ukrainians during and after the war. The Ukrainian National Alliance (the Ukrainian National Committee from late 1918), was an organization of political and humanitarian character that became the unofficial intermediary between the Ukrainian aspirations and the government in Washington.[4] At the Alliance's first general convention, held on December 25-26, 1916, in New York, the delegates representing the Ukrainian part of the exarchy, the *Soyuz,* the Providence Association, and "Zhoda Bratstv" elected Rev. Volodymyr Dovhovich the organization's first president.[5] The role of the Alliance in publicizing the Ukrainian national aspirations and providing material aid to the victims of war should not be underestimated. A major part in this work was played by the exarchy through its administrator, Father Poniatishin.

---

[2] The announcement of the organization of the Alliance was published in *Svoboda* (Jersey City, New Jersey), December 5, 1916, p. 1.

[3] Poniatishin, Peter, "Ukrainska Tserkva i U. N. Soyuz," *Propamiatna Knyha Ukrainskoho Narodnoho Soyuza, 1894-1934* (Jersey City: Ukrainian National Association, 1936), p. 293. (Hereafter cited as *Knyha Soyuza.*)

[4] A letter from a Second Assistant Secretary in the State Department to Poniatishin, chairman of the Ukrainian National Committee, dated December 16, 1918 (in reply to Father Poniatishin's letter of November 18, 1918), indicates that the State Department was glad to utilize the committee as a medium through which to acquire information regarding Ukraine, but that it was not prepared to recognize it as an official spokesman of the Ukrainian people. Letter in the Archives of the Ukrainian Museum in Chicago.

[5] Protocol from the first general convention, *America,* December 30, 1916, p. 3.

The greatest accomplishment of the Ukrainian Alliance was its work leading to the proclamation of a Ukrainian Day by President Wilson in 1917. Greatly influenced by the fact that the Jews, Lithuanians, and Armenians succeeded in obtaining a special proclamation from the President in 1916, naming a special day for the collection of funds in the United States for each of these peoples suffering as a result of the circumstances of the war, the Ukrainian Alliance decided in December of the same year to attempt a similar proclamation for the Ukrainians. The responsibility for obtaining such a proclamation was placed on the shoulders of the administrator, Rev. Poniatishin.[6]

Together with the attorney for the exarchy, William J. Kearns, Poniatishin discussed the problems with Congressman James A. Hamill of New Jersey,[7] who joined them in discussing the matter with the president's secretary, Joseph P. Tumulty, on January 4, 1917. The secretary made it clear that since similar requests were being made by endless individuals and groups, it would be impossible for the President to make such proclamations in the future. The only possibility for such a proclamation by the President, he suggested, would be an emergency resolution passed by both houses of Congress unanimously. In spite of such odds the officers of the Ukrainian Alliance went to work on effecting such a resolution.

It is interesting to note that in preparing such a resolution for Congress the question of terminology became a major problem. Rev. Poniatishin and the officers of the Committee involved in the preparation of the formal statement, held the opinion that the text of the resolution must contain the term "Ukrainian," the proper name for their people. On the other hand, Congressman Hamill, in whose Washington office the resolution was being prepared on the morning of January 24, called their attention to the fact that the term "Ruthenian" could not be omitted from the resolution, for he doubted if there were even a few Congressmen who ever heard of a people called

[6] Rev. Poniatishin discussed in detail the steps leading to the proclamation of Ukrainian Day immediately after the events took place in "Istoriia Ukrainskoho Dnia," *Svoboda,* March 31, April 3, 1917, p. 3. Many years later he again wrote about these events in "Ukrainska Sprava v Amerytsi," *Yuvileiny Almanakh Svobody, 1893-1953* (Jersey City: Ukrainian National Association, 1953), pp. 66-71. (Hereafter cited as *Almanakh Svobody.*) Both accounts are alike in substance.

[7] Congressman Hamill in his remarks in the House, on February 21, 1917, reviews the specific contacts with Father Poniatishin which brought to his attention the humanitarian objectives of the Ukrainians. See U.S., *Congressional Record,* 64th Cong., 2d Sess., 1917, LIV, Part 6 (Appendix part 1-5), 522.

"Ukrainian." This fact had to be taken into consideration by the framers of the resolution, aware that it had to be passed unanimously. They finally decided to use both terms in the text by incorporating the word *Ukrainian* in parentheses after the word *Ruthenian*. After much work by Rev. Poniatishin, his Committee, Congressman Hamill, and others, to gain Congresssional support, the resolution was finally passed by the Senate on February 7, 1917,[8] and by the House on February 22, 1917.[9] President Wilson approved the Joint Resolution of Congress on March 2, 1917, and his proclamation designating April 21, 1917, as Ukrainian Day appeared on March 16, 1917.[10] The proclamation of a Ukrainian Day by President Wilson was considered by Ukrainian leaders to be their greatest accomplishment since the beginning of Ukrainian immigration to America.[11] This was the first time that the name "Ukrainian" was used in a United States Government document,[12] and the President's proclamation represented an official public recognition by Congress and the President that there was such a people as "Ukrainians" in the world. From this time on the old name "Ruthenian" began to pass rapidly out of use in the United States and the national name of "Ukrainian" began to take its place in American usage.

At the same time that the Ukrainian Alliance was carrying on its work to obtain a Ukrainian Day, serious efforts were being made by Father Poniatishin and the Alliance to free Metropolitan A. Sheptytsky who was exiled to Russia at the beginning of the war. Poniatishin wrote to Congressman Hamill on December 27, 1916 requesting that the United States Government attempt to obtain Sheptytsky's release. In his letter Poniatishin emphasized his need of the Metropolitan's presence in the United States, and guaranteed to provide for his support as well as to bear the expense for Sheptytsky's passage to the United States by way of either Archangelsk or Norway.[13]

---

[8] U.S., *Congressional Record*, 64th Cong., 2d Sess., 1917, LIV, Part 3, 2751-2752.

[9] *Ibid.*, Part 4, 3909.

[10] U. S., *Statutes at Large*, XL, Part 2, 1645-1646.

[11] According to Father Poniatishin, American Ukrainians are indebted to Congressman Hamill, President Wilson's secretary Tumulty, attorney Kearns, and a half-dozen other Senators and Congressmen, who understood their aspirations and through whose influence the Ukrainian Day became a reality. See *Svoboda*, April 3, 1917, p. 3, and *Almanakh Svobody*, p. 76.

[12] *Almanakh Svobody*, p. 76.

[13] Copy of Father Poniatishin's letter to Congressman James A. Hamill, dated December 27, 1916. Letter in the Archives of the Ukrainian Museum in Chicago.

Congressman Hamill thought it wise to start action and together they brought the matter to the attention of the State Department. As a result, several cablegrams were written to the American Ambassadors in Vienna and St. Petersburg. With no replies forthcoming, Poniatishin and Hamill visited Tumulty, who, after a visit to the President's office, informed them that if replies were not received in three weeks the President would write personally to the Czar.[14] In the meantime the Russian Revolution broke out, the Metropolitan was released and thus American intervention in the matter ended.

After the armistice in November 1918, Rev. Poniatishin and his colleagues felt that their committees had an opportunity to aid their people in Europe by starting action in Washington towards United States recognition of the independent Ukrainian state. With the aid of Congressman Hamill, Poniatishin was given an audience with Secretary of State Robert Lansing regarding this matter. Obtaining little satisfaction, the committee prepared a memorandum to President Wilson, who headed the American Peace Delegation in Paris.[15] After the American Delegation left for Paris, Congressman Hamill brought up a joint Resolution in Congress on December 13, 1918, which if passed would have recommended that the American Delegation apply Wilson's self-determination of nations principle to the Ukrainians.[16] Although the resolution did not pass, it did inform Congress about the hopes of the Ukrainians.

The Ukrainian Alliance (now reconstituted as the Ukrainian National Committee) also sent a delegation to the Peace Conference in Paris to aid the official Ukrainian delegation from Ukraine. The motive was to aid the Ukrainian cause by influencing the American Delegation headed by President Wilson. The failure of the Ukrainians to realize their political aspirations at the Paris Peace Conference also resulted in a loss of prestige for the Ukrainian Committee in America. Thus, the committee was finally dissolved after nearly five years of fruitful activity. Through its ties with similar organizations of other stateless peoples, its various deputations, memoranda, petitions, publications, and letters, the committee had publicized the Ukrainian aspirations before the American Government and public.[17]

---

[14] *Almanakh Svobody*, p. 71.

[15] *Ibid.*, p. 73.

[16] U.S., *Congressional Record*, 65th Cong. 3d Sess., 1918, LVII, Part I, 434.

[17] The following examples illustrate the significant role of Father Poniatishin and of his committee in their attempts to bring aid to the Ukrainian people in Galicia. In a letter to the Executive Committee of the National Catholic War Council, in Washington, D.C., dated October 30, 1919, Poniatishin pointed

Writing in 1934, Father Poniatishin stated that never before or since had Americans of Ukrainian descent been so united and active in aiding the national aspirations of their people in Europe. Through its work the committee gained great respect and influence not only in the American press, educational circles, humanitarian and political organizations, but also among the political and military leaders in Washington who turned to it as the spokesman and representative of Americans of Ukrainian descent for information regarding Ukrainian matters.[18] A major force behind this work was the Church. "The Church and the *Soyuz*," states Rev. Poniatishin, "actually created the Ukrainian national movement in America and educated the masses in it. Were it not for the Church and the *Soyuz*, the greatest portion of our immigrants would have been scattered among Polish, Russian, Hungarian, and other churches and organizations, and would have been lost to the Ukrainian nation. They are two great fortresses of Ukrainian national consciousness in America."[19] In essence, Poniatishin felt it was the result of the united efforts of the Church and the *Soyuz* during the war years that Americans of Ukrainian descent began to understand that an appreciation of their national heritages was an important sign of cultural maturity.[20]

In October 1922, within a year after the dissolution of the Ukrainian National Committee, the United Ukrainian Organizations of the United States was founded under the inspiration of Dr. Luke Myshuha. Rev. Leo Levitsky became the new organization's first president. It continued the activities formerly carried on by the

out that Metropolitan Sheptytsky, the Primate of Galicia, was interned by the Polish authorities, that about 200 of his priests were held in the notorious Brigidky prison (Brigitta, the building of the former monastery of St. Brigitta) in Lviv, that relief work had not penetrated into Galicia, and again requested an investigation of conditions and aid for the Ukrainians in Eastern Galicia. In a five-page memorandum to the United States Secretary of State, dated September 7, 1920, Poniatishin vigorously complained about Polish atrocities against Ukrainian Catholics in Eastern Galicia, such as the closing of three theological seminaries, internment of bishops, and the shooting of eleven priests, and begged the United States to use its influence to put an end to these conditions. Finally a letter from the Department of Foreign Affairs of the Galician (Western Ukraine) Republic in exile, dated in Vienna, November 10, 1921, and signed by Gregory Myketey, officially thanked Poniatishin for taking the first politico-diplomatic action to inform the United States government and President Wilson about the Ukrainian viewpoint concerning Galicia. The above letters are in the Archives of the Ukrainian Museum in Chicago.

18 *Knyha Soyuza*, p. 294.
19 *Ibid.*, p. 299.
20 *Ibid.*, p. 299.

Alliance and its successor, the National Committee. The Church continued to support the new organization's efforts to aid the afflicted
in Europe.

The Ukrainians in Galicia faced grave hardships following the
war. Metropolitan Count Andrew Sheptytsky of Galicia poignantly
expressed the plight of his people in a letter of December 18, 1920
to Father Poniatishin when he wrote: "Our life is sorrow, gloom,
silence, misery, grief,—blood and tears." [21]

Having received an invitation from Poniatishin to be a formal
guest of the exarchy, the Metropolitan made his second visit to the
United States in November of 1921 primarily to seek relief for his
distressed people. The Metropolitan had two main objectives while
in the United States. He wished to collect funds for the war orphans
in Galicia, and he also hoped for an audience with President Warren
G. Harding, Secretary of Commerce Herbert C. Hoover, and Secretary
of State Charles E. Hughes, with whom he wished to discuss the
plight of the Ukrainians in Galicia. [22]

Father Poniatishin made a special request that collections be
made in all the Ukrainian Churches for the war orphans and that
they be mailed to the Metropolitan who was temporarily residing at
the late Bishop's residence in Philadelphia. On January 30, 1922, the
Metropolitan informed Poniatishin by letter that he had already
received a total of $2,534.83 from forty-two of the parishes. [23] Hardly
a church failed to contribute to this collection, with St. Joseph's in
Frankford, Pennsylvania (whose pastor was Rev. Volodymyr Petriv-
sky), contributing $900.00, the highest amount on a percentage
basis. [24] In addition, voluntary contributions were made by the clergy.
The Metropolitan also attempted to get financial aid from the Latin
Catholics during his visits to various members of the hierarchy in
whose territory Ukrainian churches were located. However, due to
postwar circumstances, aid from this quarter was hardly possible.
The American bishops were deluged with requests for aid from various European nations devastated by war; consequently, they just
could not handle the situation. For example, Monsignor Michael J.
Lavelle, pastor of New York's St. Patrick's Cathedral and a great

---

[21] Sheptytsky's letter, from Lviv, Galicia, in the Archives of the Ukrainian
Museum in Chicago.

[22] Poniatishin, "Z moikh Spomyniv," *Ukraintsi u Vilnomu Sviti: Yuvileina
Knyha Ukrainskoho Narodnoho Soyuza, 1894-1954* (Jersey City: Ukrainian National Association, n.d.), pp. 21-22. Hereafter cited as *Ukraintsi u Sviti.*

[23] Metropolitan's letter in the Archives of the Ukrainian Museum in Chicago.

[24] *Ukraintsi u Sviti*, p. 28.

friend of the Ukrainians, told Rev. Poniatishin so many requests
from Europe were received at the Chancery that to satisfy them it
would be necessary to arrange collections for every Sunday for several years in advance.[25] If the Metropolitan had arrived during the
war, or even a year earlier than he did, the entire matter of aid would
have appeared in a different light. In his recollections, written many
years after these events, Rev. Poniatishin hazarded the opinion that
upon leaving the United States the Metropolitan could not have had
more than $15,000, from all sources, for the Galician orphans.[26]

Shortly after his arrival, the Metropolitan inquired about the
possibility of an audience with Washington officials. To arrange
an audience with the President, Rev. Poniatishin turned to friends
he had made in Washington during his work leading to the Ukrainian Day proclamation in 1917. Eventually, with the aid of Senator
Frelinghuysen from New Jersey and of President Harding's Secretary, the Metropolitan, together with Rev. Poniatishin and the diocesan attorney Kearns, got to speak with the President for a few
minutes prior to his weekly public reception. During the brief audience the Metropolitan attempted to inform the President about
the harsh military occupation of Eastern Galicia by the Poles. Next,
the Metropolitan wished to see Secretary Hoover, who had been in
Lviv in the summer of that year as the American Relief Administrator. Again, Senator Frelinghuysen arranged an audience. In the presence of Poniatishin and attorney Kearns, the Metropolitan thanked
Hoover, in the name of the Ukrainian people, for the American relief in Galicia. He then brought up the question of the unfair treatment of the Ukrainian needy in the distribution of American
relief packages by the Polish occupational authorities as well as
the general political misfortune of the Ukrainians. When the audience
ended, the Metropolitan left Hoover's office in a dejected mood for
he realized, according to Poniatishin, that his visit would not result
in any substantial improvement of conditions for Ukrainians in Galicia.[27]

In March of 1922 the Metropolitan left for an extended tour
of Ukrainian colonies in Brazil and Argentina,[28] after which he re-
turned to the United States in August.[29] In October, when the Metropolitan was convalescing from his serious illness in Chicago, he re-

25 *Ibid.,* p. 28.
26 *Ibid.,* p. 30.
27 *Ibid.,* p. 27.
28 *America,* March 15 and 20, 1922, p. 1.
29 *Ibid.,* August 11, 1922, p. 1.

quested Rev. Poniatishin to arrange an audience with the Secretary
of State, Hughes.[30] Again with the help of Senator Frelinghuysen,
a meeting was arranged for early November. Accompanying the
Metropolitan to the audience were Dr. Luke Myshuha (the representative of the Western Ukrainian government in exile, who prepared a memorandum about the Polish occupation of Eastern Galicia and its persecution of the Ukrainian Church, clergy, etc.), and
attorney B. Pelekhovich. After thanking the Secretary for America's
hospitality, the Metropolitan explained the reason for the visit. He
then asked for America's influential intervention at least in the matter of the persecuted Ukrainian Church and clergy. The Secretary
promised to study the prepared memorandum carefully.

The concerted postwar effort by Metropolitan Sheptytsky, assisted by Father Poniatishin and the Ukrainian National Committee, to obtain aid for the Ukrainians in Galicia through the intervention of the American government did not succeed. On March 15,
1923, the Allied Council of Ambassadors finally decided that Eastern
Galicia be permanently attached to Poland. That decision was a
bitter blow to Ukrainian patriotic hopes. It also marked an end to
the war-phase efforts of the Ukrainian Church in America to provide moral and material aid to their less fortunate kinsmen in Europe.

---

[30] Sheptytsky's letter to Poniatishin, dated October 29, 1922, in the Archives
of the Ukrainian Museum in Chicago.

## UKRAINIAN DAY PROCLAIMED IN CHICAGO, ILLINOIS
## 1969

Mayor Richard Daley of Chicago, Illinois proclaimed the date of January 22, 1969 as Ukrainian Day in Chicago.  Here is the text of the
proclamation.

Source:  Ukrainian Congress Committee of
America. Ukrainian Independence - January
22, 1918 - Historical Background.  New York:
1974.

OFFICE OF THE MAYOR

CITY OF CHICAGO

RICHARD J. DALEY
MAYOR

P R O C L A M A T I O N

      WHEREAS, the 51st Anniversary of the Proclamation
of Independence of the Ukraine will be observed by the Chicago
Ukrainian Community on January 22nd;  and

      WHEREAS, Chicago is recognized as the United States
City where the Captive Nations movement receives its greatest
support;  and

      WHEREAS, the freedom-loving people of Ukraine have
never accepted Soviet Russia domination and have with every
means at their disposal resisted enslavement and continue to
strive for their independence:

      NOW, THEREFORE, I, Richard J. Daley, Mayor of the City
of Chicago, in demonstration of the sympathy and support which
the people of Chicago have extended and will continue to extend
to the people of the Ukraine, designate Wednesday, January 22nd
to be observed as UKRAINIAN INDEPENDENCE DAY IN CHICAGO.

    Dated this 17th day of January, A.D. 1969.

Mayor

# UKRAINIAN DAY PROCLAIMED IN NEW JERSEY
## 1970

January 22, 1970, was proclaimed as
Ukrainian Day in the state of New Jersey
by Governor William Cahill. The following is the text of the proclamation.

Source:  Ukrainian Congress Committee of
America. *Ukrainian Independence - January
22, 1918 - Historical Background*. New York:
1974.

STATE OF NEW JERSEY
Executive Department

PROCLAMATION

WHEREAS, for fifty-two years, Ukranians throughout the world have been commemorating a great and joyous day, January 22nd, 1918, for it was on this day, after
almost two hundred years of foreign domination, that they proclaimed to the world,
from St. Sophia Square, in Kiev, the ancient capital of Ukraine, that the "Independent
National Republic of Ukraine is hereby established on all Ukrainian territories;" and

WHEREAS, a great truth was established: "that any nation can fall but only a
great nation can rise again;" and

WHEREAS, the Republic had existed more than three years when it was overpowered
by superior armed forces, particularly those of communist Russia and more than forty
million Ukrainians lost their national independence; and

WHEREAS, despite this loss, the people of Ukraine have withstood many liquidations
by their communist overlords; millions of Ukrainians were systematically starved to
death in Russian planned famines of 1932 and 1933; millions more were deported to
Russian slave labor camps in Siberia; the Ukrainian Catholic and Orthodox religions have
been abolished and its religious leaders imprisoned and worked to death in far off
Siberian camps and mines; its educational system has been stripped of the Ukrainian
language; and

WHEREAS, despite all of this, the people of Ukraine struggle on in the hope that
their nation will somehow be liberated from communist oppression and restored to the
Ukrainian people; and

WHEREAS, in order that encouragement shall be given to these brave people by
the people of America, and that Ukrainians and Americans of Ukrainian descent be afforded
the opportunity of formally commemorating the significance of this memorable day
throughout the State of New Jersey;

NOW, THEREFORE, I, WILLIAM T. CAHILL, Governor of the State of New Jersey, do
hereby proclaim

JANUARY 22, 1970

as

UKRAINIAN INDEPENDENCE DAY

in New Jersey and urge our citizens to make appropriate observance of the occasion.

GIVEN, under my hand and the Great Seal
of the State of New Jersey, this
twenty-second day of January in
the year of Our Lord one thousand
nine hundred and seventy and in
the Independence of the United
States the one hundred and ninety-
fourth.

GOVERNOR   *William Cahill*

## YEARLY UKRAINIAN INDEPENDENCE DAY REQUESTED
## 1970

In July and August, 1970, Congressmen Kleppe
and Schweiker introduced two resolutions,
House Resolution No. 1127 and Senate Resolution No. 455, requesting that the president
of the United States be authorized to designate January 22nd of each year as Ukrainian
Independence Day.  Both resolutions were referred to the Committee of the Judiciary.
Their text follows below.

Source:  Ukrainian Congress Committee of
America.  Ukrainian Independence - January
22, 1918 - Historical Background.  New York:
1974.

91st CONGRESS
2d Session

# H. RES. 1127

---

## IN THE HOUSE OF REPRESENTATIVES

JULY 1, 1970

Mr. KLEPPE submitted the following resolution; which was referred to the Committee on the Judiciary

---

# RESOLUTION

Whereas Ukraine, with a population of forty-seven million, is the
largest non-Russian nation both in the Union of Soviet Socialist Republics and in Eastern Europe; and

Whereas this nation occupies a significant geographic and economic position in the context of Eurasia, with prominent
dimensions toward central Asia, the Caucasus, the Middle
East, and central Europe; and

Whereas this second largest Slavic people, with a national history extending back to the ninth century, has made substantial contributions to world culture and today possesses immense potentialities and promise for further universal cultural advancement; and

Whereas, in partial recognition of these cultural contributions toward civilization and peace, the Eighty-sixth Congress of these United States of America passed the Shevchenko Memorial resolution, leading to the erection of a statue of Taras Shevchenko, the poet laureate of Ukraine, on public grounds in our Nation's capital; and

Whereas the critical importance of this non-Russian nation in world affairs has been obliquely reflected in the original charter membership of the Union of Soviet Socialist Republics; that is, the Ukrainian Soviet Socialist Republic, in the United Nations; and

Whereas for the past two decades the Congress, Governors of our major States, and mayors in our largest cities have consistently observed the indomitable spirit of independence and creative assertions of the Ukrainian people; and

Whereas the independent Ukrainian National Republic, which was established by democratic, popular vote and national self-determination on January 22, 1918, was one of the first to proclaim freedom for its people in the area of the traditional Russian Empire: Now, therefore, be it

1    *Resolved*, That the President is authorized and re-
2    quested to issue a proclamation designating January 22 of
3    each year (the anniversary of the proclamation which de-
4    clared Ukraine to be a free and independent republic) as
5    Ukrainian Independence Day, and inviting the people of
6    the United States to observe such day with appropriate
7    ceremonies.

91st CONGRESS
2D SESSION
# S. RES. 455

---

# IN THE SENATE OF THE UNITED STATES

August 25, 1970

Mr. Schweiker submitted the following resolution; which was referred to the Committee on the Judiciary

# RESOLUTION

To designate January 22 as Ukrainian Independence Day.

Whereas Ukraine, with a population of forty-seven million, is the largest non-Russian nation both in the Union of Soviet Socialist Republics and in Eastern Europe; and

Whereas this nation occupies a significant geographic and economic position in the context of Eurasia, with prominent dimensions toward central Asia, the Caucasus, the Middle East, and central Europe; and

Whereas this second largest Slavic people, with a national history extending back to the ninth century, has made substantial contributions to world culture and today possesses immense potentialities and promise for further universal cultural advancement; and

Whereas, in partial recognition of these cultural contributions toward civilization and peace, the Eighty-sixth Congress of these United States of America passed the Shevchenko Memorial resolution, leading to the erection of a statue of Taras Shevchenko, the poet of Ukraine, on public grounds in our Nation's capital; and

Whereas the critical importance of this non-Russian nation in world affairs has been obliquely reflected in the original charter membership of the U.S.S.R.; that is, the Ukrainian Soviet Socialist Republic, in the United Nations; and

Whereas the contemporary status of Ukraine has been reflected in the Captive Nations Week Resolution passed by the Eighty-sixth Congress in July 1959, and signed by President Dwight D. Eisenhower into Public Law 86–90; and

Whereas for the past two decades the Congress, Governors of our major States, and mayors in our largest cities have consistently observed the indomitable spirit of independence and creative assertions of the Ukrainian people; and

Whereas the independent Ukrainian National Republic, which was established by democratic, popular vote and national self-determination on January 22, 1918, was one of the first to proclaim freedom for its people in the area of the traditional Russian Empire: Now, therefore, be it

1    *Resolved*, That the President is authorized and requested
2 to issue a proclamation designating January 22 of each
3 year (the anniversary of the proclamation which declared
4 Ukraine to be a free and independent republic) as Ukrainian
5 Independence Day, and inviting the people of the United
6 States to observe such day with appropriate ceremonies.

VERKHOVYNA
A UKRAINIAN AMERICAN RESORT CENTER
1970

The following is a short article describ-
ing the history and development of a
Ukrainian American resort center in the
Catskill Mountains.

Source: Forum: A Ukrainian Review,
Spring, 1970.

CRADLED BY THE STATES of New York, New
Jersey, and Pennsylvania, the Ukrainian Workingmen's Association's *Verkhovyna* Resort Center
has become one of the exceptionally delightful va-
cationlands in the Catskill Mountains. The land-
scape in which *Verkhovyna* lies is unique in its
beauty and variety. On one side of Lake Verkhovyna, the Hotel and Castle Guest House are resplen-
dent amidst a dark green of woods which stretch
for many miles through gentle, hilly country. On
the other side of the thirteen acre lake, imposing
buildings form an essential part of the Hotel galaxy
formed by small boulevards whose intimate aspect
is provided by romantic lanes.

Purchased in 1955, the UWA was intent on
acquiring vacationland property for its membership.
The Verkhovyna site was chosen because it was
tailored to a Carpathian type of environment—a
paradise two thousand feet above sea level on one
hundred and sixty acres of green meadows, mountain valleys, orchards, gardens, and plateau pasture-
land with a multi-species forest which affords a
breathtaking panorama of the surrounding country-
side. In a pleasant climate with a view of natural
inland scenery the embracing entrance along the
bridged Delaware River is indeed a wondrous
depth of beauty that belongs to *Verkhovyna*.

The *Verkhovyna* hospitality has a well founded
name where guests are treated royally and within no
time advance to the status of honored friends. The
modern restful rooms are coupled with a Ukrainian
cuisine that meets every culinary expectation. The
rates are lower than the neighboring spas offering
similar facilities — and UWA members are treated

to discounted charges.

The "social town" concept cultivated by the
UWA has a network of activities that services all
age levels. The children's camp and summer cultural courses are professionally staffed and provide
the Ukrainian kind of environment that meets par-
ental objectives. All guests are serviced at Lake
Verkhovyna, at an olympic-size swimming pool,
soccer field, tennis courts, all which give the optimum
energetic releases through sporting events. There
is an excellent pavilion for dancing and presentation of cultural projects.

THE RESTORATION and renovation program has
been a fundamental commitment of the UWA
personnel with the needs of visitors and guests
placed as the main focus of attention. The continuous but sophisticated presentation of cultural-artis-
tic events throughout the summer exemplifies the
wealth of intellectual intensity. Choruses, singers,
musicians, humorists, actors, and dancing groups
are bountiful and sparkle with brilliance each week-
end.

Into this mountainous wonderland region there
has been a steady influx of Ukrainian neighbors,
many who have already established permanent resi-
dencies. With a population of approximately seven
hundred and fifty people, this wealth of spotted
homes in a terrain of grandeur has enriched the
real estate values. One of the most impressive land-
marks is the unusual architecturally styled church—
the Catholic St. Volodymyr. The completion of this
grandiose edifice could not have been possible without the generous land grant to this group by the
UWA. The memorial grave Brody-Lev across from
St. Volodymyr Church is another UWA land do-
nation dedicated to the valiant men and women who
have given their lives in Ukraine's struggle for
nationhood.

The UWA's ambitious programs have an aura
of expectancy that excites the imagination — with
an optimism that *Verkhovyna* will ultimately become the greatest and most outstanding Ukrainian
Resort in America — a home for senior citizens, a
Ukrainian Orthodox Church, library, Ivan Franko
Museum, a Taras Shevchenko monument are only

a part of the total agenda.

The UWA Resort Center is a fulfillment of an important goal and marks a tremendous achievement on this 60th Anniversary year. The services which have been rendered to the general Ukrainian population through a vacationland medium should be recognized as humanitarian — and it becomes incumbent for all Ukrainians to join this fraternal to enhance the attainment of proposed goals. Yes — the honor and glory of the past belongs to the pioneers and dedicated UWAites—but with faith, hope, and charity, the future of Verkhovyna will emerge as the most productive and prosperous Ukrainian vacationland center to contain the fine traditions of our founding fathers.                    ▼

SHEVCHENKO SCIENTIFIC SOCIETY CENTENNIAL
1973

In 1973 the Shevchenko Scientific Society
of America celebrated a century of creative
existence, prolific publishing activity,
and useful exchange of ideas and experiences
with three sister societies:   the Shevchenko
Scientific societies of Canada, Europe, and
Australia.  The following is a brief description of the Shevchenko Scientific Society of
America with headquarters in New York City.

Source:   Wasyl, Professor Lew.  A Century
of Dedicated Work for Scholarship and Nation.
New York:   Shevchenko Scientific Society in
the United States, 1973.

*The Shevchenko Scientific Society of the United
States* (American, or AShSS) with headquarters in New
York City, which sprang out of the branch of the Society
founded by Prof. Dr. Nicholas D. Chubaty, owns its building, purchased under the direction of Prof. Chubaty, and
serves as the "House of Ukrainian Culture." The building was purchased in 1955, the mortgage loan being provided by the "Providence" Association of Ukrainian
Catholics. It contains the Library, the office of the executive secretary (at present Roman Kobrynsky), and a
conference room. Half of the premises is leased to the
Ukrainian Congress Committee of America (UCCA), thus
easing some of the financial obligations of the Society.

The *Library of the American Shevchenko Scientific
Society* has 4,808 books, 7,249 periodicals and 327 small
manuscripts — all in all 12,384 items. The Library was
established through the generosity of its patrons, such as
the previously mentioned V. Doroshenko and Prof. V.
Miyakovsky, and the following: a) Dr. Neonila Pelekho-
vich-Hayvoronsky, who donated 682 books of her late
husband, composer Mykhaylo Hayvoronsky; b) Professor
Matthew Stachiw who donated 599 books; c) Very Rev.
Lev Chapelsky (560 books); d) the late Professor Roman
Smal-Stocki (268 books); e) Bohdan Zahaykevych (160
books); f) Antin Malanchuk of New Haven, Conn, (490
books); it also purchases new books.

In addition, smaller quantities of books came from several other donors; others have come from various institutions on an exchange basis. The executive board of the American Shevchenko Scientific Society also collects Ukrainian classics. (A .detailed report on donors nid Poltava (librettos of *Anna Yaroslavna* and *Lys Mykyta)*, Dr. Rostyslav Lepky (part of the archives of Prof. Bohdan Lepky), E. Faryniak of Chicago (letters of M. Hrushevsky), the archives of the Shevchenko Memorial Committee of Argentina, and the Ukrainian group in Aschaffenburg (Soviet documents relative to the confiscation of private holdings and the establishment of the collective farm system), and others.

The present executive board of the American Shevchenko Scientific Society consists of the following:

Matthew Stachiw — President, (former Presidents: N. Chubaty, R. Smal-Stocki);

Joseph Andrushkiw — 1st Vice President; Nicholas Chirovsky — 2nd Vice President; Peter Stercho, Ivan Kedryn-Rudnytsky and Edward Zarsky — Vice Presidents; Basil Steciuk — Scientific Secretary; Roman Kobrynsky — Executive Secretary and Treasurer;

Representatives of Sections: Wasyl Lew (Philological Section); Joseph Andrushkiw (Mathematical-Physical Section); Mykola Zaytsev (Chemical-Biological-Medical Section); Stepan Horak (Section on the History of Ukraine).

*Delegates* to the Supreme Council of the Shevchenko Scientific Society: P. Stercho, Gregory Luznycky.

*Members-at-large:* Lidia Burachynska, Mykola Bohatiuk, Rev. Meletius Wojnar, OSBM, Bohdan Hnatiuk, Walter Dushnyck, Imre Kardashinets, Wasyl Lencyk, Gregory Luznycky, Vincent Shandor;

*Deputy Members-at-large:* Petro Bohdansky, Sviatoslav Trofimenko, Alexander Luznycky, Yuriy Kulchytsky and Alexander Sokolyszyn;

*Auditing Committee:* Jaroslaw Padoch, Michael S. Pap, Antin Dragan, Ivan Nowosiwsky and Ivan Zukovsky.

In the United States the Society has the headquarters of the Philological, Mathematical-Physical and the Chemical-Biological-Medical Sections and the Section on the

History of Ukraine. The Society's Centers are located in: of books and money appears in *Naukove Tovarystvo im. Shevchenko v ZDA,* New York, 1960).

The *Archives of the American Shevchenko Scientific Society* consist of the generous donations of the following:

Prince Ivan Tokarzevsky-Karashevych and Prof. Alexander Lototsky (both collections were donated by Dr. Borys Veligost-Lototsky), Prof. O. Kalynyk, Prof. I. Pasichniak, Dr. Sophia Parfanovych, Dr. Antin Rudnytsky (musical score of the opera *Anna Yaroslavna),* Leo-Washington (head: Yuriy Starosolsky), Philadelphia (head: Roman Maksymovych), Cleveland (head: I. Slavnychy) and Detroit (head: A. Shutka).

The American Society has 100 full members, 17 members-correspondents, 223 ordinary members and 19 members-sympathizers.

HARVARD UKRAINIAN RESEARCH INSTITUTE
1973

The Harvard Ukrainian Research Institute
was established in June, 1973, as a result of a joint endeavor made by more
than 8,000 individual contributors.  The
main purpose of the institute is the training of new scholars in the area of Ukrainian studies.  The following are selected
aspects regarding the institute's history,
courses, publishing program, and library
collections.

Source:  Ukrainian Studies at Harvard:
Cambridge, Massachusetts:  Ukrainian
Studies Fund, 1974.

## HISTORY

Ukrainian Studies at Harvard had its beginning in 1957, when students at the Congress of the Federation of Ukrainian Student Organizations of America (SUSTA) in Cleveland discussed the necessity for preserving and continuing
the development of Ukrainian scholarship. It was determined that the best way to attain this goal would be through
the endowment of a chair in Ukrainian studies at a major American university.

By 1967, $280,000 had been raised for the undertaking by the Ukrainian Studies Fund, specifically organized for
this purpose (see section entitled "The Capital Drive"). At that time, the Fund approached Prof. Omeljan Pritsak of
Harvard University for advice on how best to utilize the raised capital. Prof. Pritsak was invited to head the Council of
Academic Advisers, a body of Ukrainian professors from various American colleges and universities, which negotiated
with Columbia University, the University of Minnesota and Harvard University. After discussions with President
Nathan M. Pusey and Dean of the Faculty of Arts and Sciences Franklin L. Ford, the Council proposed Harvard as
the university best suited for a program of Ukrainian studies because of its strong tradition in Eastern European
and Soviet studies.

Additional funds were raised to meet the $600,000 endowment required for each chair at Harvard. On January 22,
1968, an exchange of letters between President Pusey and Stephan Chemych, President of the Ukrainian Studies Fund,
formalized the agreement establishing a chair in Ukrainian history at Harvard University. The effort resulting in this
achievement received warm praise from Dean Ford: "I found it rather moving to consider the genesis of this particular
endowment and the launching of this particular fund, because it seemed to me to combine what a university should
combine: the interest and impulse of young people with the traditions and cultural heritage that people of all ages
must not want to be lost...The Ukrainian effort is unique in my experience up until now in the level of student
involvement."

After the initial transfer of funds which established the chair in Ukrainian history, Dean Ford appointed the
Committee on Ukrainian Studies to supervise and coordinate a program of Ukrainian studies. A plan was formulated
to include the following developments: the endowment of two additional chairs in Ukrainian literature and language;
the inauguration of a publishing program; the expansion of library collections; the introduction of Ukrainian courses
at the Harvard Summer School; and the establishment of a research institute.

During the academic year 1968—69, courses in Ukrainian studies were offered by several Harvard departments.
Ad hoc programs of study were set up to prepare a new generation of scholars in Ukrainian studies. Funds were al-
located for the expansion of library holdings, and the first volume of the Harvard Series in Ukrainian Studies was
published.

# DOCUMENTS 111

Five years after the establishment of the first chair in Ukrainian Studies at Harvard, a transfer of funds from the Ukrainian Studies Fund to the new President of Harvard University, Derek C. Bok, marked the endowment of the chairs in Ukrainian literature and language. This event was officially observed on April 30, 1973, with the public defense of the dissertation of Orest Subtelny, the first written under the auspices of the Committee on Ukrainian Studies. To assure international standards in the evaluation of this dissertation, the defense committee included Prof. Pritsak and Prof. Edward L. Keenan of Harvard University, Prof. Oleksander Ohloblyn, formerly of the State University of Kiev, and Prof. Józef Gierowski of the Jagiellonian University of Krakow.

On this occasion, President Bok expressed Harvard's commitment to the Ukrainian Studies Program: "We are proud to have been selected as the university to carry on the scholarly traditions of Ukraine in this country. We are touched by the broad support that members of the Ukrainian community have given to this undertaking. We take this support as a mandate to do our best to foster learning and scholarship relating to the language, literature and history of Ukraine."

The Harvard Ukrainian Research Institute was established in June of 1973. During the first decade of its operation, the main objective of the Institute is to conduct basic research projects and to provide annotated bibliographies and teaching materials for the three major Ukrainian disciplines. Professors on sabbatical leave from other universities and qualified researchers have been invited to cooperate in this effort with the associates of the Harvard Ukrainian Research Institute.

All major activities of the Harvard Ukrainian Studies Program are reported in the monthly *Newsletter* of the Committee on Ukrainian Studies.

## COURSES AND SEMINARS

The activities of the Ukrainian Studies Program at Harvard began soon after its official inauguration. During the academic year 1968—69, arrangements were made with the Departments of History and Slavic Languages and Literatures for courses in Ukrainian studies to be taught within these departments. Prof. Oleksander Ohloblyn was invited to become the first Visiting Lecturer in Ukrainian history, an appointment which was extended through the following academic year. Courses in Ukrainian language and literature were taught by Harvard faculty, assisted by graduate students. Since then, Ukrainian literature courses have been offered by the Department of Comparative Literatures.

Ukrainian Studies offers a minimum of two courses in history, two in language, and one in literature each semester. Students are able to receive a master's or doctoral degree from the departments mentioned with concentration in Ukrainian disciplines. Flexible programs are designed for each student on an individual basis by these departments and the Committee on Ukrainian Studies. Informal conferences and tutorials are also provided to supplement programs of study.

In the fall of 1970, a weekly Seminar in Ukrainian Studies was established to serve as a school of methodology and as a regular forum for the exchange of scholarly information. Graduate students associated with Ukrainian Studies at Harvard and guests from other universities are invited to discuss their research, methodology and the sources of their materials. At times, two or more speakers deal with a particular problem. Such was the case in March 1974, when Prof. Peter Reddaway of the London School of Economics and Political Science, Prof. Thomas

E. Bird of Queens College, and Prof. Alexander Yesenin-Volpin of Boston University examined the political and religious aspects of the dissident movement in Soviet Ukraine. Presentations at the Seminar have focused on such disciplines as history, archival research, political science, economics, literary criticism, philology, linguistics, archeology, demography and urban studies. Reports of the Seminar are published at the end of each academic year in the *Minutes of the Seminar in Ukrainian Studies*.

Occasional special lectures are also sponsored by Ukrainian Studies. During March of 1971, Dr. Jurij Bojko-Blochyn of the Ludwig-Maximillian University in Munich delivered a series of lectures on the poetess Lesja Ukrajinka.

Since the second semester of the 1972–73 academic year, Ukrainian Studies has offered a noncredit, weekly seminar dealing with an intensive textual study of *Povest' Vremennyx Lĕt (The Nestor Chronicle)* — the major historical and literary source of early Ukrainian history. This seminar is conducted by Prof. Horace G. Lunt, with the participation of Profs. Edward L. Keenan, Omeljan Pritsak and Ihor Ševčenko.

With the change in status of the Committee on Ukrainian Studies, new courses will be sponsored directly by the Committee and all seminars will be given for academic credit.

## THE PUBLISHING PROGRAM

From its inception, Ukrainian Studies at Harvard has placed great emphasis on the development of a comprehensive program of scholarly publications.

The Harvard Series in Ukrainian Studies, published by Wilhelm Fink Verlag of Munich, includes reprintings of old works as well as original studies and translations. The Series is edited by the Committee on Ukrainian Studies, with Prof. Omeljan Pritsak acting as Editor-in-Chief. Since 1969, seven titles have appeared in print:

Fedir Savčenko, *The Suppression of Ukrainian Activities in 1876,* 415 pp (1969)
George S. N. Luckyj, *Between Gogol' and Ševčenko,* 210 pp (1971)
Oleksander Ohloblyn, *A History of Ukrainian Industry,* 1197 pp (1971)
*Eyewitness Chronicle* (Litopys Samovydcja), edited by Orest Levyc'ky, 468 pp (1972)
Myron Korduba, *La littérature historique sovietique ukrainienne,* LVI, 365 pp (1972)
*The Galician-Volynian Chronicle,* translated and introduced by George Perfeckyj, 196 pp (1973)
Dmitrij Tschiževskij, *Skovoroda: Dichter, Denker, Mystiker,* 233 pp (1974)

Harvard Ukrainian Studies is also involved in the preparation of teaching materials in Ukrainian language, literature and history. Prof. Horace G. Lunt heads the group of scholars working on a language textbook. Bohdan Krawciw is preparing a bibliographical survey of Ukrainian literature in the 20th century. Prof. Pritsak and Prof. Ihor Ševčenko are working on a textbook of Ukrainian history up to 1648; the sequel to this work, dealing with Ukrainian history through modern times, is being prepared by Dr. Orest Subtelny.

The semiannual journal — *Recenzija: A Review of Soviet Scholarly Publications* — examines current Soviet Ukrainian works in the humanities and social sciences, as well as scholarly periodicals in these areas. Review articles are written by graduate students associated with Ukrainian Studies at Harvard, with occasional contributions from Harvard faculty and scholars from other universities. Students are also responsible for the editing and distribution of the journal. The editors of *Recenzija* are appointed on a rotating basis; Prof. Pritsak serves as faculty adviser. Eight issues of *Recenzija* have been published since the fall of 1970. In his review of the journal, Prof. John S. Reshetar, Jr. of the University of Washington writes: "...*Recenzija* has set a high standard not only for Soviet Ukrainian scholarship but for its contributors as well. The high quality of the contributions prepared by advanced graduate students associated with the Harvard Ukrainian Studies Program bears testimony to its exacting standards." (*Slavic Review,* vol. 33, no. 3, p. 558, September 1974).

At the end of each academic year, Ukrainian Studies at Harvard publishes a report of the Seminars held during the course of that year. The *Minutes of the Seminar in Ukrainian Studies* include synopses of each presentation and discussion, bibliographical materials pertaining to each presentation, and an index of speakers and topics. The *Minutes* are published by the Committee on Ukrainian Studies, with graduate students acting as editors on a rotating basis. Four issues of this publication have appeared since its inception during the academic year 1970–71.

Work has begun on an annual journal — *Harvard Ukrainian Studies* — to be published under the auspices of the Harvard Ukrainian Research Institute, with Profs. Pritsak and Ševčenko serving as Editors-in-Chief. This publication will concentrate on developing an interdisciplinary approach to Ukrainian studies. It will contain an extensive bibliographical section and a chronicle of scholarly events.

Beginning with the year 1974—75, Ukrainian Studies will provide bound offprint copies of articles published by the associates of the Ukrainian Research Institute in scholarly journals. The first issue of this reprint series will consist of a study by Dr. Paul R. Magocsi, "An Historiographical Guide to Subcarpathian Rus'," scheduled to appear in the *Austrian History Yearbook*. The American Council of Learned Societies has awarded the Institute a special grant to cover the costs of reprinting this work.

All publications of the Ukrainian Studies Program at Harvard are available to libraries, institutions and private subscribers.

## THE LIBRARY COLLECTIONS

The development of the Ukrainian collections at Harvard long preceded the establishment of the Ukrainian Studies Program at this university. The accelerated and systematic building of the collections began in 1968, when the Committee on Ukrainian Studies appropriated subsidies for additional acquisitions and a full-time librarian. As a result, Ucrainica at Harvard today stands among the largest of any major university library collection.

A great portion of the collections was acquired through gifts. One of the most outstanding collections donated to Harvard was that of Bayard L. Kilgour, Jr. in the 1950's. Among the more recent gifts were the library of the Ukrainian archeologist Jaroslaw Pasternak, donated by his widow in 1970, and the library and archives of Michael Bazansky, donated in 1974.

The Ukrainian collections have also been expanded by purchase and through exchanges. The first major purchase — in 1957 — was the library of the Ukrainian journalist Mykola Ceglinsky, which consisted of some 800 titles, primarily in Ukrainian history, politics and government. Since 1968, Harvard has been purchasing microfilms and photocopies of works not obtainable in the original. In 1969, agreements were reached for the exchange of publications between the Harvard College Library and the library of the Ukrainian Academy of Sciences in Kiev, the Lenin Library in Moscow and the Leningrad Public Library.

The major concentration of Ucrainica is housed in the Widener Memorial Library and the Houghton Rare Books and Manuscripts Library. The Harvard University Library System is comprised of over ninety specialized libraries — such as the Cabot Science Library, the Law School Library and the Fogg Art Museum Library — and many of these also contain minor Ukrainian collections. Jaryna A. Turko is the librarian responsible for the building and cataloguing of these collections.

The Houghton Library affords the finest possible security for rare Ucrainica. Among some of the titles found in this library are the *Apostol* and *Primer*, the first books printed in Ukraine by Ivan Fedorov (L'viv, 1574); the Edicts

of Hetman Ivan Mazepa; the manuscript of Hryhorij Skovoroda's *Dialogue*; and many first editions of such classics of Ukrainian literature as Ivan Kotljarevs'kyj, Taras Ševčenko and Pantelejmon Kuliš. An exceptionally interesting item is the first edition of Myxajlo Maksymovyč's *Malorossijskija pesni*, since the copy in the Harvard collections belonged to Taras Ševčenko, as is confirmed by Pantelejmon Kuliš on a preliminary leaf of the book.

In October of 1970, the Ukrainian Seminar Library was opened in Widener Library to serve as a reference collection primarily for historians. Lubomyr A. Hajda serves as curator of this library.

Since September 1973, Ukrainian reference works are also housed in the library of the Harvard Ukrainian Research Institute. This library, set up under the direction of Edward Kasinec, is an integral part of the Harvard University Library System and is subordinate to the libraries of the Faculty of Arts and Sciences. Starting with fewer than 100 volumes, through gifts, purchases and exchanges with other Slavic libraries, the library has expanded to thousands of volumes.

The collection of the Reference Library includes encyclopedias; dictionaries; national bibliography; specialized bibliographies of monographs and serials;

complete works of major authors; guides to collections of published and unpublished documentation; guides to learned societies and institutions; classic textbooks in the humanities; and offprints of contemporary scholarship on Ukraine and works of Ukrainian scholars in all disciplines. The library also serves as a center for reserve materials for the various courses, seminars and tutorials offered by the Ukrainian Studies Program.

In addition to these services, the Reference Library is compiling a catalogue of Ucrainica in the Harvard University Library System and lists of the various gifts to the Ukrainian collections which have been placed in specialized libraries of the University. The Reference Library will also undertake several major bibliographical projects: compiling retrospective indices to Ukrainian serials; maintaining a current bibliography of emigré Ucrainica; and reprinting classic works in Ukrainian bibliography.

Harvard Ukrainian Studies has sponsored a number of library exhibits to acquaint the University community and the general public with the Ukrainian collections. The first of these, held at the Widener and Houghton Libraries in December 1970 and January 1971, presented a survey of Ukrainian scholarship from the earliest times to the present. An exhibit featuring Ukrainian manuscripts, early prints and rare books was displayed at the Widener Library in the spring of 1973 to observe the establishment of the three chairs in Ukrainian Studies at Harvard. Creativity among Ukrainians in displaced persons camps from 1945 to 1950 was the subject of a third exhibit in May and July of 1974. A display of rare books from the Ukrainian collections was organized for the benefit of the students participating in the 1974 Ukrainian Summer School session at Harvard.

# THE UKRAINIAN NATIONAL ASSOCIATION
## 1974

On February 22, 1974 the Ukrainian National Association, the oldest, most numerous, and most influential of Ukrainian American organizations, celebrated its eightieth anniversary. Here is a short history of the Ukrainian National Association.

Source: Svoboda, The Ukrainian Weekly, (February 23, 1974).

JERSEY CITY, N.J. — As this issue of the Ukrainian Weekly was being printed, the Ukrainian National Association's newly constructed 15-story skyscraper, named "Ukrainian Building" was dedicated in noon ceremonies Friday, February 22, the exact day of the Association's 80th anniversary.

Hundreds of specially invited guests, including clergy, federal, state and local officials, representatives of Ukrainian national organizations, as well as all members of the Supreme Asembly and many area UNA'ers, took part in the impressive ceremonies.

### Anthems in Ukrainian

The program began at noon with the singing of the American, Canadian and Ukrainian anthems. The national anthems were sung in the Ukrainian language by a chorus composed of UNA and Svoboda employees, conducted by Osyp Stecura.

The American hymn was translated by the late Dr. Semen Demydchuk, and the Ukrainian version of "Oh Canada!"

### Statistics Not Enough

Indeed, today's Soyuz is a far cry from what it was in the early beginnings. But here the applicability of comparative statistics no longer suffices to unravel the full story of growth, progress and, most of all, service that the organization has rendered over the years to its members, to the Ukrainian community and our struggling kinsmen in Ukraine.

What has made it all possible is a determinant, a constant that cannot be measured in physical terms, a spark that was kindled in that little church hall in Shamokin eighty years ago, which has mushroomed into an all-embracing flame that runs with burning zeal through the history of Soyuz: it is the spirit of courage, determination, idealism, and self-denying effort that knew the ultimate reward in the total good of others. It was the spirit of the Ukrainian pioneers, manifested in their foresight and a desire for unity, that launched the UNA, sustained it over the years, and helped overcome the periodic crises which no organization can escape. They provided the spiritual tools, as it were, for thousands of men and women that followed in their footsteps, adhering to the ideals of fraternalism and Ukrainianism whose seeds were sown and whose meaning defined in the small yet festively decorated church hall in Shamokin eighty years ago.

It was this spirit that was translated into myriad of concrete accomplishments that make the UNA not only the oldest, but also the largest, the strongest and the most influential Ukrainian organization in the free world. And it is this spirit that runs its triple streak through the organization's history: service to its members, service to the entire community, service to the Ukrainian people. It is the ideal blending of a business enterprise and a community oriented organization that has laid the foundations of Ukrainian organized life in this country and has done its share in preserving and fostering Ukrainian heritage and identity.

### True Cross-Section

Today the UNA embraces Ukrainians of all walks of life, of all ages, professions and religious faiths, thus constituting a true cross-section of our community. With 460 branches in 28 states of this country and seven provinces of Canada, there is hardly an outpost of Ukrainian life from the Atlantic to the Pacific that does not have a group of UNA'ers as its backbone. With its total membership now closing in on 90,000, its total assets nearing 40 million

dollars, its total insurance in force having passed the 140 million dollar plateau, the UNA is an organization that is a credit to all Ukrainians. It stands out as a pragmatic example of the Ukrainian ability to organize and manage their affairs, and apply the amassed assets in service to the community.

Apart from its periodical publications — the Svoboda daily, The Ukrainian Weekly, the children's magazine "Veselka" — the UNA has brought out a series of books on Ukraine, capping this type of service by financing the publication of the two-volume "Ukraine: A Concise Encyclopaedia" in English. A project realized by the UNA at a cost of over $300,000, the encyclopedia has been acknowledged as the best reference source on Ukraine in the English language.

UNA's commitment to and involvement in the community life has found its tangible expression in such vast projects as the establishment of a Center of Ukrainian Studies at Harvard, the erection of the Taras Shevchenko Monument in Washington, D.C., the convocation of the World Congress of Free Ukrainians. In these and other projects of lasting significance, the UNA, collectively and individually, has played a leading role.

It has been said that the UNA is our largest youth organization. With over 24,000 members in its Juvenile Department, this fact can hardly be disputed. But more than that: from some $40,000 awarded over the past decade in scholarships to young Ukrainians to the promotion of educational, cultural and athletic programs—with the participation of thousands of young people at Soyuzivka, a place that they have learned to call their own — the UNA is pursuing in the very spirit of the pioneers who launched the organization not so much for themselves but for their progeny.

Remarkable as the input of the UNA is, it is accomplished with a membership that represents but 5 percent of the total estimated Ukrainian population on the North American continent. How much more could be done, how much stronger our Ukrainian power base would be if the majority of Ukrainians were in the active ranks of the organization that has the tools for growth and the momentum of progress.

In its eightieth year, the UNA can justly flaunt its record of service and achievement. In the years and decades ahead, let us help embellish that record.

## UKRAINIAN LANGUAGE IN MARYLAND
### 1975

An interesting article regarding the ac-
ceptance of the Ukrainian language as a
credit subject in high schools was recently published by Paul Fenchak, chairman of
the Ukrainian Education Association of
Maryland. The article is reproduced below.

Source: Forum: A Ukrainian Review, no.
28, 1975.

DURING THE 1973-74 ACADEMIC YEAR the
Ukrainian Language was accepted as a subject to be studied for credit towards graduation
from high school by the Maryland State Department of Education. Ann A. Beusch, Specialist in Foreign Languages for the Maryland
Department of Education, has indicated that
credit for out-of-school programs in Ukrainian
is now being granted by five school systems in
Maryland: Baltimore City, Howard, Montgomery, Prince George's and Anne Arundel Counties. Under existing provisions students living in
other school areas could be granted credit for
the study of Ukrainian language with the con-
sent of the local school system. Previously programs for language credit in high schools existed
only for the study of Hebrew and Greek in
Maryland, Ukrainian being the first Slavic language to be given credit status.

The drive to receive accreditation for Ukrain-
ian in the Baltimore area was led by Wolodymyr
C. Sushko, Assistant Principal of the School of
Ukrainian Studies-Ukrainian Congress Commit-
tee of America, who is also an instructor in a
Baltimore School. Working with Mr. Sushko
were Principal Mychajlo Choma and Instructor
Lidia Lemischka, along with the Parents' Com-
mittee of the School, chairman of which is Mr.
Theodore Chay.

Rev. George Markewych, in his first year as
pastor of Sts. Peter and Paul Ukrainian Catholic
Church, Curtis Bay, Maryland, contributed
greatly to the success of the School's program by
instructing the students in the subject of

religion.

THE SCHOOL OF UKRAINIAN Sciences operates during the regular school year from 9:00 a.m. until 2:00 p.m. on Saturdays. The enrollment this past year was 35 students in secondary grades. Classes are held at the Ukrainian Self-Reliance Association Building, 239 S. Broadway, Baltimore. Subjects studied in the school include geography, history, language, literature, culture.

Baltimore's school was the second Ukrainian school in Maryland to be accredited by the State, the first being the Ukrainian School in Montgomery County. All of the instructors in the Baltimore School are fully certificated by the Maryland Department of Education, and on the strength of the faculty, the program of studies, and good results, the School recently received full certification by the State.

Mr. Sushko believes that the record of success for the perpetuation and recognition of Ukrainian studies in Maryland is worthy of similar advancement in other Ukrainian communities in the United States. "We Ukrainians have much to add to the American cultural storehouse," he says, "but first we must learn to operate effectively in American society so that we, as others, get full benefit of all government services — most important of which is education."

Paul Fenchak, *Chairman*

Ukrainian Education Assoc. of Maryland
2301 Eastern Avenue
Baltimore, Maryland 21224 ▼

UKRAINIAN AMERICANS SALUTE
AMERICA'S BICENTENNIAL
1975

On September 21, 1975 thousands of Ukrainian Americans representing different cities,
organizations, and generations, saluted our
country's Bicentennial and the one hundredth
anniversary of the Ukrainian mass settlement
in the United States. An interesting pam-
phlet regarding the above event was distribu-
ted by the Ukrainian Bicentennial Committee.
Here are some of the relevant pages.

Source: Ukrainians Salute Bicentennial of
American Revolution. Ukrainian Bicentennial
Committee of America and United Committee of
Ukrainian Organizations of New York, 1975.

## FELLOW AMERICANS!

The Ukrainian American community, over 2 million strong, located in
every State of the Union—from the Atlantic to the Pacific and from the
Canadian to the Mexican borders—salutes the Bicentennial of American
Independence and joins with millions of other Americans in observing this
great historical event in a truly heartfelt and meaningful manner.

## HISTORICAL RETROSPECT

Ukrainians in the United States are not late-comers to these shores of
freedom. Although there is evidence of the presence of Ukrainians in
America during the Colonial Period and that some fought in the
Revolutionary and Civil Wars, the bulk of them came here in four successive
immigration waves:

From 1865-1890, 1895-1914, 1920-1939 and 1946-1955.

The actual arrival of Ukrainians in America in substantial numbers
began in 1865-1875. Therefore, along with the observance of the Bicentennial of the American Revolution, we also celebrate the 100th Anniversary of
the Ukrainian Settlement in America.

## DISTRIBUTION IN AMERICA

Oppressed by Czarist Russia and exploited by the Austro-Hungarian
Empire and by successive foreign governments which kept Ukraine in subjugation, Ukrainians had good reason to emigrate overseas. America, the

land of freedom and opportunity, beckoned irresistibly.

Here, in America:

- They swelled the industrial force by settling in the coal mining areas of Pennsylvania, Ohio, West Virginia and Illinois·
- In the iron ore regions of Minnesota and Michigan;
- In the gold and silver districts of Montana and Colorado;
- In the farm states of Nebraska and the Dakotas;
- Some went as far as the West Coast: California, Oregon and Washington; while hundreds found their way to Texas, Oklahoma and Louisiana;
- Thousands of them made their homes in the metropolitan areas of New York, Philadelphia, Chicago, Cleveland, Detroit and other urban areas.

## TRANSFORMATION OF UKRAINIAN AMERICAN SOCIETY

Today, the Ukrainian American community has assumed a more equitable distribution with respect to means of livelihood and pursuits. The early distinguishing characteristics of a laboring class have given way to a diversity of callings, including the professions and business.

The second and third generations and some 100,000 new Ukrainian immigrants who arrived in the period after World War II have expanded the professional lists considerably.

**Thousands of Ukrainian Americans are scientists, doctors, dentists, college and university professors, engineers, journalists, priests, musicians, commercial artists, bankers, teachers, veterinarians, librarians and students.**

**Others are employees in city, state and federal posts, or members of the U.S. Army, Navy, Air Force and the Marine Corps, as well as city and state police forces.**

**Thousands are industrialists, merchants, building contractors, hotel, motel and restaurant owners, importers and exporters, owners of small retail and large commercial concerns, factories and so forth.**

## UKRAINIAN AMERICAN COMMUNITY

The Ukrainians and their progeny have devleoped, in the course of the 100 years of their settlement in America, a thriving ethnic community and, while they are loyal Americans, they continue to cultivate their ethnic heritage, including their native language, national and cultural traditions and their religion.

Their dynamic life is manifested in a variety of forms and expressions, which include:

- **Religion:** The Ukrainian Catholic Church, with a metropolitan and three bishops; the Ukrainian Orthodox Church, with a metropolitan, an archbishop and a bishop; and the Ukrainian Evangelical and Baptist congregations—are the main religions;

- **Fraternal Associations:** There are four Ukrainian American fraternal associations with a combined membership of 130,000 and 59 million dollars in assets;

- **Banks and Credit Unions:** Several Ukrainian American banks and credit unions were established in the last two decades, with a combined capital of 119 million dollars;

- **Educational Institutions:** There is a Ukrainian academy of science, a scientific society, a Catholic college, a seminary and two high schools; 65 Ukrainian-language Saturday schools; three chairs of Ukrainian studies at Harvard University; the Ukrainian language, history and literature are taught at some 15 American colleges and universitites;

- **Women's, Youth and Veteran Organizations:** There exist several Ukrainian women's organizations, youth associations, sports clubs and veterans' groups;

- **Professional Associations:** There are several Ukrainian professional associations of doctors and dentists, engineers, veterinarians, university professors, lawyers, journalists and librarians;

- **Music, Dance and the Arts:** In addition to ballet schools, there exist several dozen Ukrainian choir and dance ensembles; Ukrainian artists, sculptors, actors, singers and musicians are part of American cultural life;

- **Social and Political Organizations:** Other forms of Ukrainian life are expressed in a number of Ukrainian social and political organizations, as well as in cultural and charitable institutions;

- **The Press and Book Publishing:** There are over 90 Ukrainian-language publications—2 daily newspapers, weeklies, semi-monthlies, monthlies and quarterlies, including a number of bilingual and English-language publications;

- **The Ukrainian Congress Committee of America (UCCA)** is the representative organization of the whole Ukrainian American community;

• **U.S. Broadcasts in Ukrainian:** For the past 25 years the "Voice of America," an official agency of the U.S. Government, and "Radio Liberty," a private American institution, have been broadcasting in Ukrainian to the captive people of Ukraine.

**For several generations the Ukrainians in America have given their sweat, blood, toil and talents to the growth and development of this land, and have helped to make America great and prosperous.**

**Thousands of Ukrainians served in the U.S. Armed Forces in the Spanish-American War, World Wars I and II, in the Korean and Vietnamese Wars, and thousands of them made the supreme sacrifice by giving their lives for America!**

## THE UKRAINIAN HOMELAND

### FELLOW AMERICANS!

Ukrainian Americans hail from Ukraine, a country in the southeastern part of Europe. It embraces a total of 289 square miles, rich in natural resources. The Ukrainian people are an old and historically established Slavic nation. They have had three distinct periods of independence: ·

1) The first period, known as Kievan Rus (the "Princely Era"), from the IXth to the XIVth centuries;
2) The Kozak period from the middle of the XVIth to the end of the XVIIIth centuries;
3) The modern, or third period, beginning with the fall of Czarist Russia and the Austro-Hungarian Empire in 1917-1918 and ending in 1920, when the Ukrainian National Republic was conquered by Communist Russia.

**The independence of Ukraine was proclaimed on January 22, 1918 in Kiev.**

At present, Ukraine, renamed by Moscow the "Ukrainian Soviet Socialist Republic," is a "union republic" of the USSR and a charter member of the U.N. It is not a government of the Ukrainian people, but a Russian-imposed puppet regime. The 50 million Ukrainians are captive people who suffer political and cultural oppression, economic exploitation and unbearable Russification. In 1971-1972 alone the KGB arrested over 600 Ukrainian intellectuals, men and women, for their devotion to their Ukrainian language and culture, and for their desire to see their country free and independent.

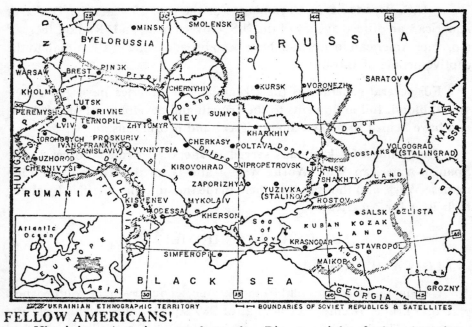

UKRAINIAN ETHNOGRAPHIC TERRITORY    BOUNDARIES OF SOVIET REPUBLICS & SATELLITES

## FELLOW AMERICANS!

Ukrainian Americans salute the Bicentennial of the American Revolution with pride and gratitude for the freedom and opportunities they have found here.

They believe the same freedom and opportunities should be enjoyed by their kin in captive Ukraine, and are striving to help them in achieving these goals. It was the Ukrainian poet laureate, Taras Shevchenko, who in one of his poems in 1857, wrote:

> " . . . When will we get our own Washington,
> With a new and righteous law?
> And get him we will . . . "

Ukrainian Americans say, "Thank you, America"—may you grow and prosper for long ages to come! Mnohaya lita!

**UNITED COMMITTEE OF
UKRAINIAN ORGANIZATIONS OF
NEW YORK
UKRAINIAN BICENTENNIAL COMMITTEE
OF AMERICA**

**September, 1975**
302 West 13th Street
New York, N.Y. 10014
Tel. (212) 924-5617

BIBLIOGRAPHY

BIBLIOGRAPHY

PRIMARY SOURCES

Honcharenko, Agapius, ed. The Alaska Herald Svoboda. The first bi-
    lingual newspaper (English and Russian) edited by the first
    Ukrainian reverend and one of the most distinguished Ukrainian
    American intellectuals during 1868 to 1872. Some materials of
    the newspaper were devoted to Ukrainians.

United States War Department. The War of the Rebellion. A Compila-
    tion of the Union and Confederate Armies. Washington, D. C.:
    G.P.O., 1880-1902. A multi-volume set in which one can find
    several pages reflecting the acts of bravery committed by Ukrain-
    ian Americans.


GENERAL BIBLIOGRAPHY

Halich, Wasyl. Ukrainians in the United States. Chicago, Illinois:
    University of Chicago Press, 1937. Basic book with substantial
    coverage on the character and number of Ukrainian immigration,
    home background, distribution in the United States, religious
    and cultural life, organizations, press, old culture vs. new
    environment. Extensive bibliography.

Hutchinson, E. P. Immigrants and Their Children: 1850-1950. New
    York: John Wiley & Sons, Inc., 1956. Brings to light impor-
    tant social and economic aspects of Ukrainian immigration in
    connection with and comparison to other ethnic groups. Based
    on the official 1950 United States Census data.

Kuropas, Myron B. The Ukrainians in America. Minneapolis, Minnesota:
    Lerner Publications Company, 1972. Good background on the
    Ukrainian way of life, and the contributions made by the Ukrain-
    ians to the United States. Designed for teenagers, but also
    good for the average layman.

Kubijovic, Volodymyr, ed. Ukraine: A Concise Encyclopedia. Toronto,
    Canada: University of Toronto Press, 1963. Two volume set pre-
    pared by the Shevchenko Scientific Society. Excellent reference
    source on the Ukraine and the Ukrainians, with extensive cover-
    age on the Ukrainian Americans as well as other Ukrainian com-
    munities from abroad.


SPECIAL BIBLIOGRAPHY

Arts and Music

Dmytriw, Olya. Ukrainian Arts. New York: Ukrainian Youth League

---

of North America, Inc., 1958. A compilation of articles by Ukrainian American scholars covering architecture, music, fine arts, embroidery, folk dress, rug making, Easter egg decorations, ceramics and wood carving.

## Biographies

Luciw, Theodore. Father Agapius Honcharenko: First Ukrainian Priest in America. New York: Ukrainian Congress Committee of America, 1970. A scholarly, very good biography on a great Ukrainian American. Relevant documents, illustrations, and extensive bibliography.

## Cooking

Stechishin, Savella. Traditional Ukrainian Cookery. Winnipeg, Canada: Trident Press, 1959. A good presentation of Ukrainian cookery, accompanied by a description of Ukrainian life and customs.

## Organizations

Fisk, Margaret, et al., ed. Encyclopedia of Associations. Detroit, Michigan: Gale Research Company, 1975. Lists Ukrainian American organizations, and describes their specific activities.

Wynar, Lubomir, ed. Directory of Ethnic Organizations. Littleton, Colorado: Libraries Unlimited, Inc., 1975. Very good coverage on Ukrainian American organizations.

## Periodicals

Wynar, Lubomir, ed. Encyclopedic Directory of Ethnic Newspapers and Periodicals in the United States. Littleton, Colorado: Libraries Unlimited, Inc., 1972. Annotates all Ukrainian American periodicals and newspapers.

## Poetry

Andrusyshen, C. H., ed. The Ukrainian Poets: 1189-1962. Toronto, Canada: University of Toronto Press, 1963. A selection of translations of Ukrainian poetry during nine centuries.

## Radio Stations

American Council for Nationalities Service. Foreign Language Radio Stations in the United States. New York: 1970. Lists all radio stations broadcasting Ukrainian language programs.

## Religion

Jaquet, Constant H. Yearbook of American and Canadian Churches: 1974. Nashville, Tennessee: Abingdon Press, 1974. Furnishes up to date statistical data on the denominations to which Ukrainian Americans belong, as well as the way they are organized.

Mead, Frank S., ed. Handbook of Denominations in the United States. Nashville, Tennessee: Abingdon Press, 1970. Describes the organizational structure of the Ukrainian Orthodox and Catholic churches.

Ukrainian Language and Linguistics Study

Bidwell, Charles E. The Language of Carpatho-Ruthenian Publications in America. Pittsburgh, Pennsylvania: University Center for International Studies, 1971. Examines the Carpatho-Ukrainian dialect in relation to the Ukrainian language.

Pei, Mario. The World Chief Languages. New York: S. F. Vanni, 1946. A noted linguist's view on the linguistic structure of the Ukrainian language, and its place in the family of Slavic languages.

Podvesko, M. Ukrainian-English Dictionary. New York: Saphrograph Company, 1963. Easy to use basic dictionary.

_____. English-Ukrainian Dictionary. New York: A.B.I.H., 1951. Easy to use basic dictionary.

Shklanka, E. Ukrainian Primer. New York: Knyho-Spilka, 1962. Fundamentals of Ukrainian, elementary level.

Slavutych, Iar. An Introduction to the Ukrainian Language. Edmonton, Alberta: Slavuta Publishers, 1962. Easy introduction to reading, writing, speaking, and understanding Ukrainian.

Stechishin, J. Ukrainian Grammar. Winnipeg, Canada: Trident Press, 1951. Basics for students learning the Ukrainian language.


PERIODICAL LITERATURE

Ceglinsky, Nicholas. "How the Ukrainians Came," The Interpreter, (January, 1924).

Danys, Tekla. "Ukrainian Christmas," San Francisco Teachers Bulletin, (December, 1934).

Dobriansky, Lev. "Ukrainian Rivulets in the Stream of American Culture," Ukrainian Quarterly, vol. lV (Winter 1948).

Halich, Wasyl. "Ukrainian Farmers in the United States," Agricultural History, January, 1936).

_____. "Ukrainians in Western Pennsylvania," Western Pennsylvania Historical Magazine, (June 1935).

APPENDICES

APPENDIX 2

UKRAINIAN AMERICAN INSTITUTIONS & ORGANIZATIONS

ASSOCIATION OF AMERICAN YOUTH OF UKRAINIAN DESCENT
    144 Parker Avenue
    Maplewood, New Jersey 07040

FEDERATION OF UKRAINIAN STUDENT ORGANIZATIONS OF AMERICA (SUSTA)
    2 East 79th Street
    New York, New York 10021

HOLY UKRAINIAN AUTOCEPHALUS ORTHODOX CHURCH IN EXILE
    Holy Trinity Cathedral Church
    185 South 5th Street
    Brooklyn, New York 11211

LEAGUE OF AMERICANS OF UKRAINIAN DESCENT
    841 North Western Avenue
    Chicago, Illinois 60622

LEMKO ASSOCIATION
    556 Yonkers Avenue
    Yonkers, New York 10704

ORGANIZATION FOR DEFENSE OF FOUR FREEDOMS FOR UKRAINE
    505 East 10th Street
    New York, New York 10003

ORGANIZATION FOR REBIRTH OF UKRAINE (ORU)
    Post Office Box Cooper Station
    New York, New York 10003

PROVIDENCE ASSOCIATION OF UKRAINIAN CATHOLICS IN AMERICA
    817 North Franklin Street
    Philadelphia, Pennsylvania 19123

SELFRELIANCE ASSOCIATION OF AMERICAN UKRAINIANS
    98 Second Avenue
    New York, New York 10003

SHEVCHENKO SCIENTIFIC SOCIETY
    302-304 West 13th Street
    New York, New York 10014

UKRAINIAN ACADEMY OF ARTS AND SCIENCES IN THE UNITED STATES
    206 West 100th Street
    New York, New York 10025

UKRAINIAN AMERICAN LEAGUE
    85 East 4th Street
    New York, New York 10003

UKRAINIAN ARTIST'S ASSOCIATION IN THE UNITED STATES (OMUA)
    c/o Ukrainian Art and Literary Club
    149 Second Avenue
    New York, New York 10003

UKRAINIAN AUTOCEPHALUS ORTHODOX CHURCH IN THE UNITED STATES
    2710 Iowa Street
    Chicago, Illinois 60622

UKRAINIAN BAPTIST CONVENTION IN THE UNITED STATES
    247 East Poland Road, Parkside
    Chester, Pennsylvania 19015

UKRAINIAN BYZANTINE RITE CATHOLIC CHURCH
    Chancery Office
    161 Glenbrook Road
    Stamford, Connecticut 06902

UKRAINIAN CONGRESS COMMITTEE OF AMERICA (UESA)
    302 West 13th Street
    New York, New York 10014

UKRAINIAN EASTERN RITE CATHOLIC CHURCH
    St. Nicholas Diocese
    2203 West Chicago Avenue
    Chicago, Illinois 60622

UKRAINIAN EASTERN RITE CATHOLIC CHURCH
    Chancery Office
    815 North Franklin Street
    Philadelphia, Pennsylvania 19123

UKRAINIAN EVANGELICAL ALLIANCE OF NORTH AMERICA
    22146 Kelly Road East
    Detroit, Michigan 48021

UKRAINIAN INSTITUTE OF AMERICA
    2 East 79th Street
    New York, New York 10021

UKRAINIAN LIFE COOPERATIVE ASSOCIATION
    2534 West Chicago Avenue
    Chicago, Illinois 60622

UKRAINIAN MEDICAL ASSOCIATION OF NORTH AMERICA
    2 East 79th Street
    New York, New York 10021

UKRAINIAN MUSEUM ARCHIVES, INC.
    4176 Spring Crest Drive
    Cleveland, Ohio 44144

UKRAINIAN NATIONAL AID ASSOCIATION OF AMERICA
      527 Second Avenue
      Pittsburgh, Pennsylvania 15219

UKRAINIAN NATIONAL ASSOCIATION (UNA)
      81-83 Grand Street
      Jersey City, New Jersey 07302

UKRAINIAN NATIONAL WOMEN'S LEAGUE OF AMERICA
      4936 North 13th Street
      Philadelphia, Pennsylvania 19141

UKRAINIAN NATIONAL YOUTH FEDERATION
      2315 West Chicago Avenue
      Chicago, Illinois 60622

UKRAINIAN ORTHODOX CHURCH IN AMERICA
      St. Andrew's Ukrainian Orthodox Diocese
      90-34  139th Street
      Jamaica, New York

UKRAINIAN ORTHODOX CHURCH OF U.S.A.
      South Bound Brook,
      New Jersey 08880

UKRAINIAN RESEARCH AND INFORMATION INSTITUTE
      2534 West Chicago
      Chicago, Illinois 60622

UKRAINIAN WORKINGMEN'S ASSOCIATION
      440 Wyoming Avenue
      Scranton, Pennsylvania 18503

UKRAINIAN YOUTH LEAGUE OF NORTH AMERICA
      602 Fanshawe Street
      Philadelphia, Pennsylvania 19111

UNITED UKRAINIAN AMERICAN RELIEF COMMITTEE
      5020 Old York Road
      Philadelphia, Pennsylvania 19141

WESTERN UKRAINE BYZANTINE RITE CATHOLIC CHURCH
      Munhall Chancery Office
      54 Riverview Avenue
      Pittsburgh, Pennsylvania 15214

WORLD FEDERATION OF UKRAINIAN STUDENT ORGANIZATIONS OF MICHNOWSKY (TUSM)
      Post Office Box 141
      Riverton, New Jersey 08077

UKRAINIAN AMERICAN PERIODICALS

AMERYKA
817 North Franklin Street
Philadelphia, Pennsylvania
19123

ANNALS OF THE UKRAINIAN ACADEMY
OF ARTS AND SCIENCES
206 West 100th Street
New York, New York 10025

BIBLOS
238 East Sixth Street
New York, New York 10003

EKRAN
Screen Illustrated
2102 West Chicago Avenue
Chicago, Illinois 60622

FENIKS
Post Office Box 141
Riverton, New Jersey 08077

FORUM: A UKRAINIAN REVIEW
440 Wyoming Avenue
Scranton, Pennsylvania

HOLOS LEMKIVSCHYNY
417 Nepperhan Avenue
Yonkers, New York 10703

KRYLATI
315 East Tenth Street
New York, New York 10009

NARODNA VOLYA
524 Olive Street
Scranton, Pennsylvania 18509

NASHA BATKIVSHCHYNA
133 East Fourth Street
New York, New York 10003

NASHA ZHYTTIA
4936 North 13th Street
Philadelphia, Pennsylvania
19141

NOVI NAPRIAMY
140-142 Second Avenue
New York, New York 10003

OVYD
2226 West Chicago Avenue
Chicago, Illinois

SHLAKH
805 North Franklin Street
Philadelphia, Pennsylvania
19123

SVOBODA
81-83 Grand Street
Jersey City, New Jersey 07303

THE UKRAINIAN QUARTERLY
302 West 13th Street
New York, New York 10014

THE UKRAINIAN WEEKLY
81-83 Grand Street
Jersey City, New Jersey 07303

UKRAINSKA KNYHA
4800 North 13th Street
Philadelphia, Pennsylvania
19141

UKRAINSKE NARODNE SLOVO
Post Office Box 1948
Pittsburgh, Pennsylvania
15230

UKRAINSKE PRAVOSLAVNE SLOVO
Post Office Box 495
South Bound Brook, New Jersey
08880

UKRAINSKYI FILATELIST
80-73 87th Avenue
Woodhaven,
Jamaica, New York 11421

UKRAINSKYI ISTORYK
Post Office Box 312
Kent, Ohio 44240

VESELKA
81-83 Grand Street
Jersey City, New Jersey 07303

## THE UKRAINIAN ALPHABET AND ITS ENGLISH PRONUNCIATION

А а - like Art

Б б - like Book

В в - like Visit

Г г - like HElmet

Д д - like Dog

Е е - like Ebony

Є є - like Yellow

Ж ж - like pleaSure

З з - like Zero

І і - like machIne

Ї ї - like bEEr

Й й - like boY

К к - like Kelp

Л л - like Lemon

М м - like Motor

Н н - like Noon

О о - like Ox

П п - like Pen

Р р - like Red

С с - like Sort

Т т - like Train

У у - like mOOn

Ф ф - like Fog

Х х - like KHaki

Ц ц - like caTS

Ч ч - like lunCH

Ш ш - like SHare

Щ щ - like miSCHief

Ь ь - indicates palatization of a preceeding consonant

Ю ю - like YUle

Я я - like YAk

## UKRAINIAN COURSES IN AMERICAN UNIVERSITIES

CATHOLIC UNIVERSITY OF AMERICA
    Washington, D. C. 20017

COLUMBIA UNIVERSITY
    New York, New York 10027

HARVARD UNIVERSITY
    Cambridge, Massachusetts
    02138

UNIVERSITY OF AKRON
    Akron, Ohio 44325

UNIVERSITY OF ILLINOIS
    Urbana, Illinois 61801

UNIVERSITY OF PENNSYLVANIA
    Philadelphia, Pennsylvania
    19104

UKRAINIAN LANGUAGE DECLARED AS MOTHER TONGUE BY
NATIVITY, PARENTAGE AND RACE

| YEARS | TOTAL | NATIVES OF NATIVE, FOREIGN BORN, OR MIXED PARENTAGE | FOREIGN BORN |
|-------|-------|------------------------------------------------------|--------------|
| 1910  | 35,359  | 10,228  | 25,131 |
| 1940  | 80,820  | 45,280  | 35,540 |
| 1970  | 249,351 | 152,716 | 96,935 |

UNITED STATES CENSUS - 1970

|  | TOTAL | WHITE | OTHER RACES |
|--|-------|-------|-------------|
| TOTAL | 249,351 | 248,665 | 501 |
| NATIVE OF NATIVE PARENTAGE | 22,662 | 22,584 | 27 |
| NATIVE OF FOREIGN OR MIXED PARENTAGE | 130,054 | 129,787 | 208 |
| FOREIGN BORN | 96,635 | 96,294 | 266 |

Source: U. S. Department of Commerce. 1970 Census of Population: Detailed Characteristics - U.S. Summary. Washington, D. C.: U. S. Government Printing Office, 1973.